The Repetitious Coloring Book

Illustrations by Curtis W. Jackson

This is a gift for:

....

From

....

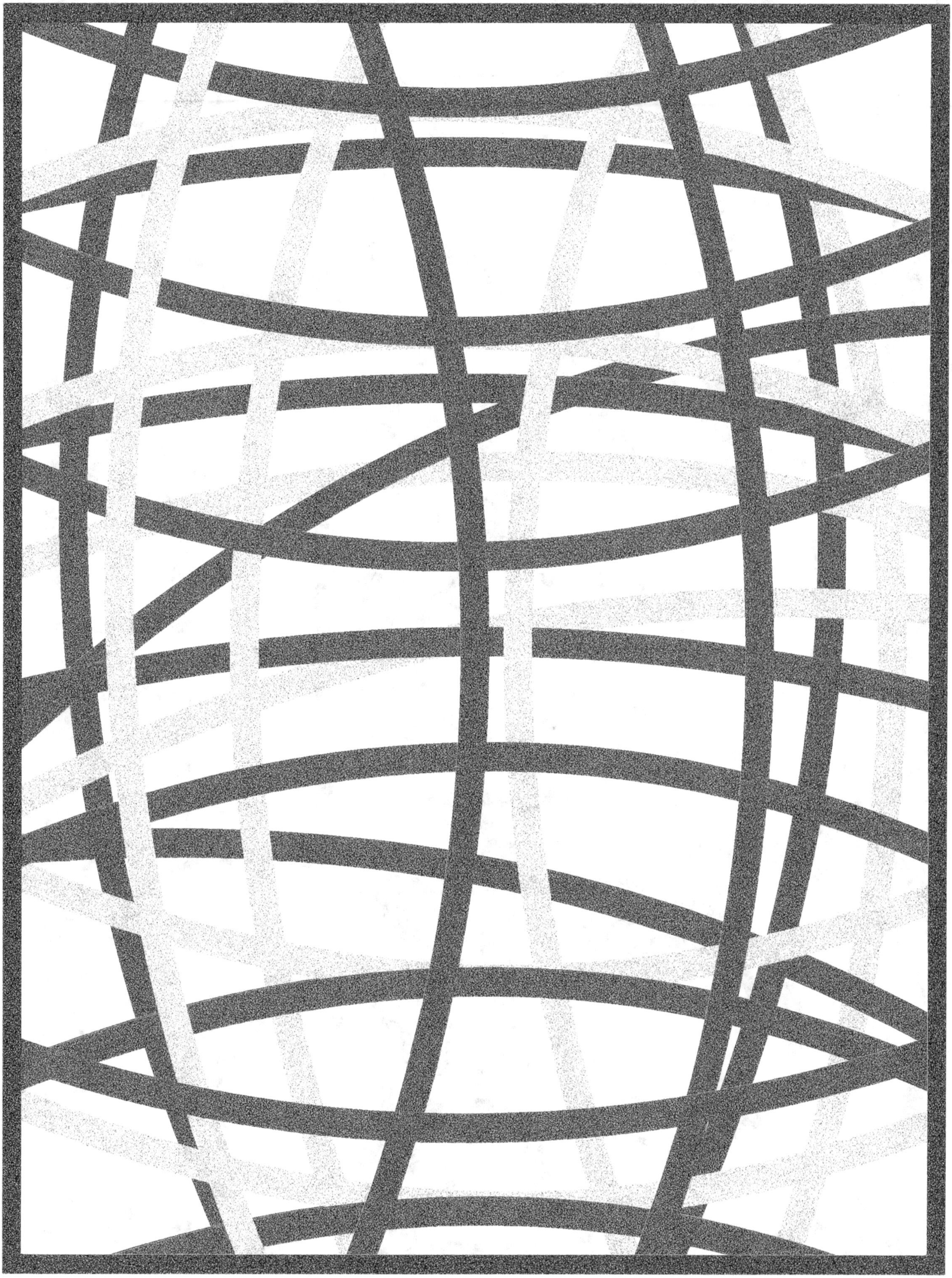

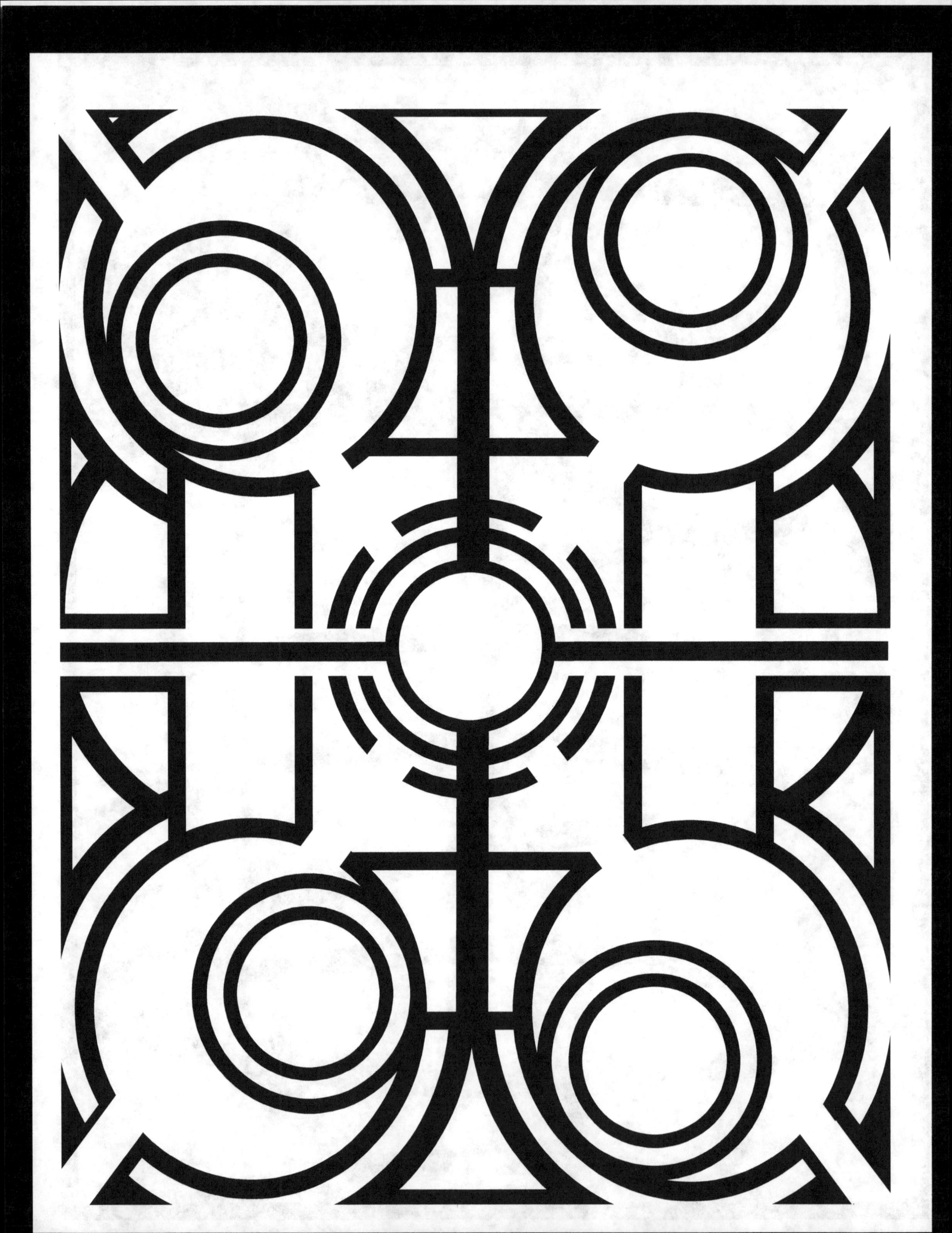

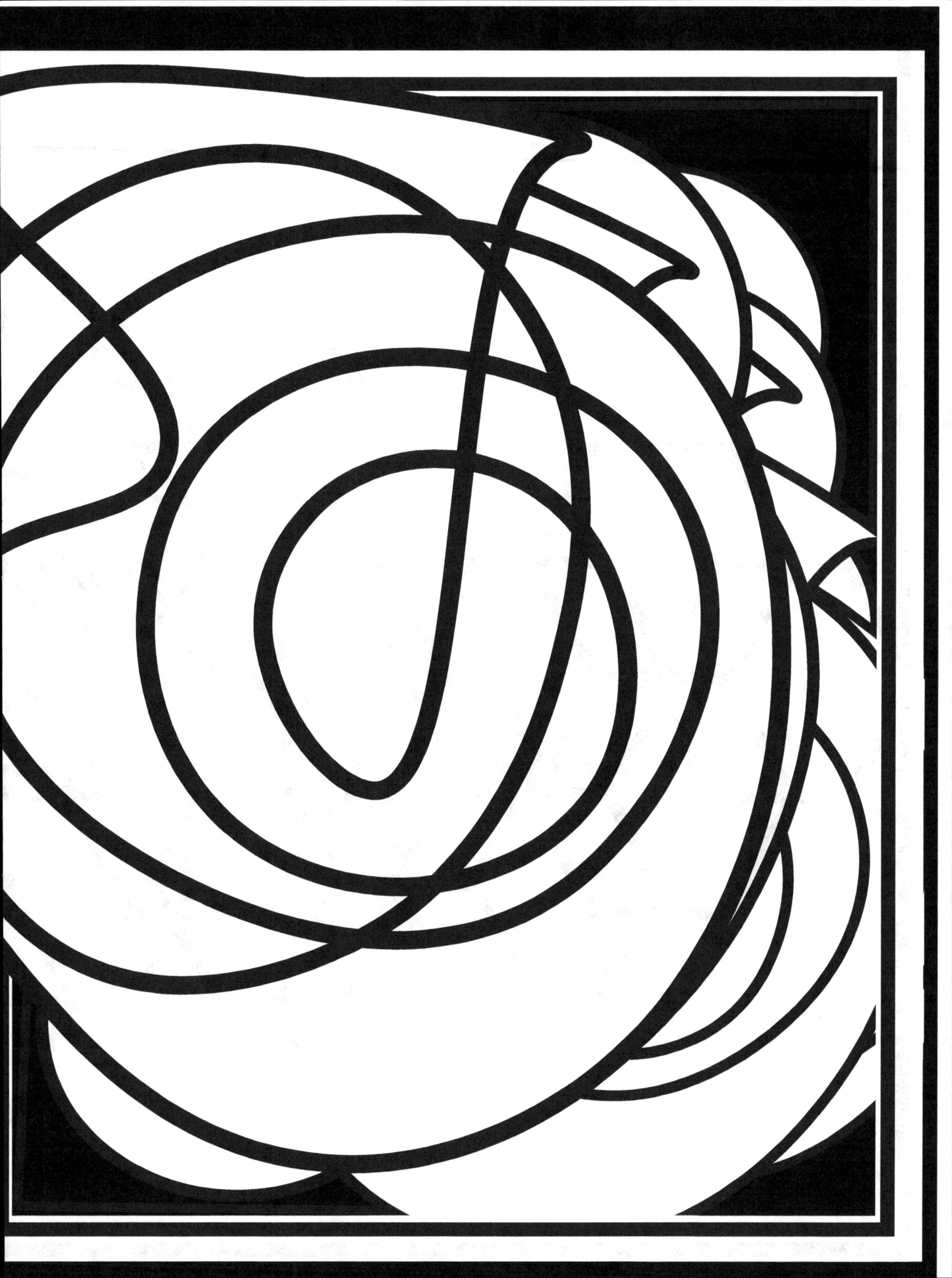

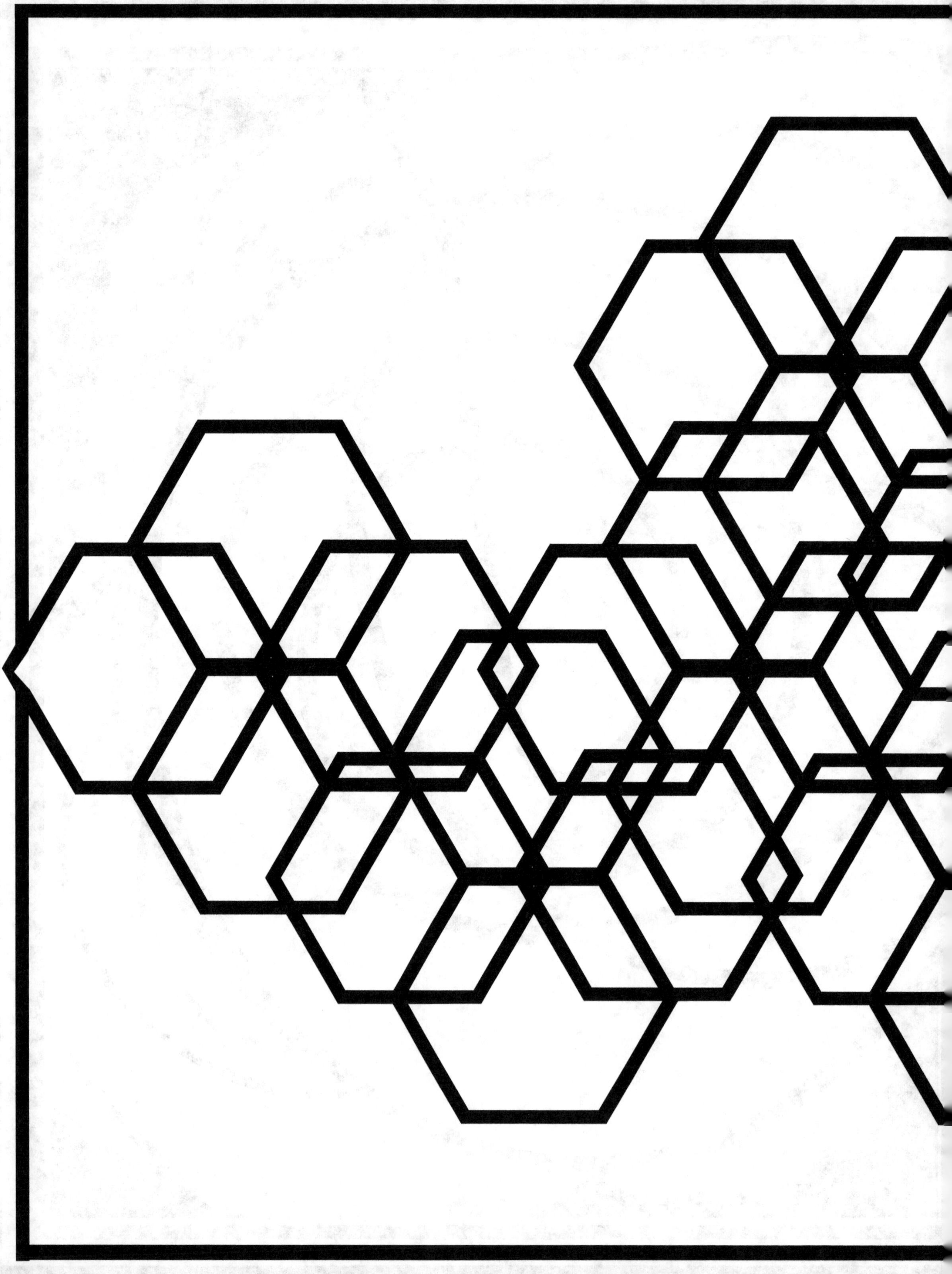

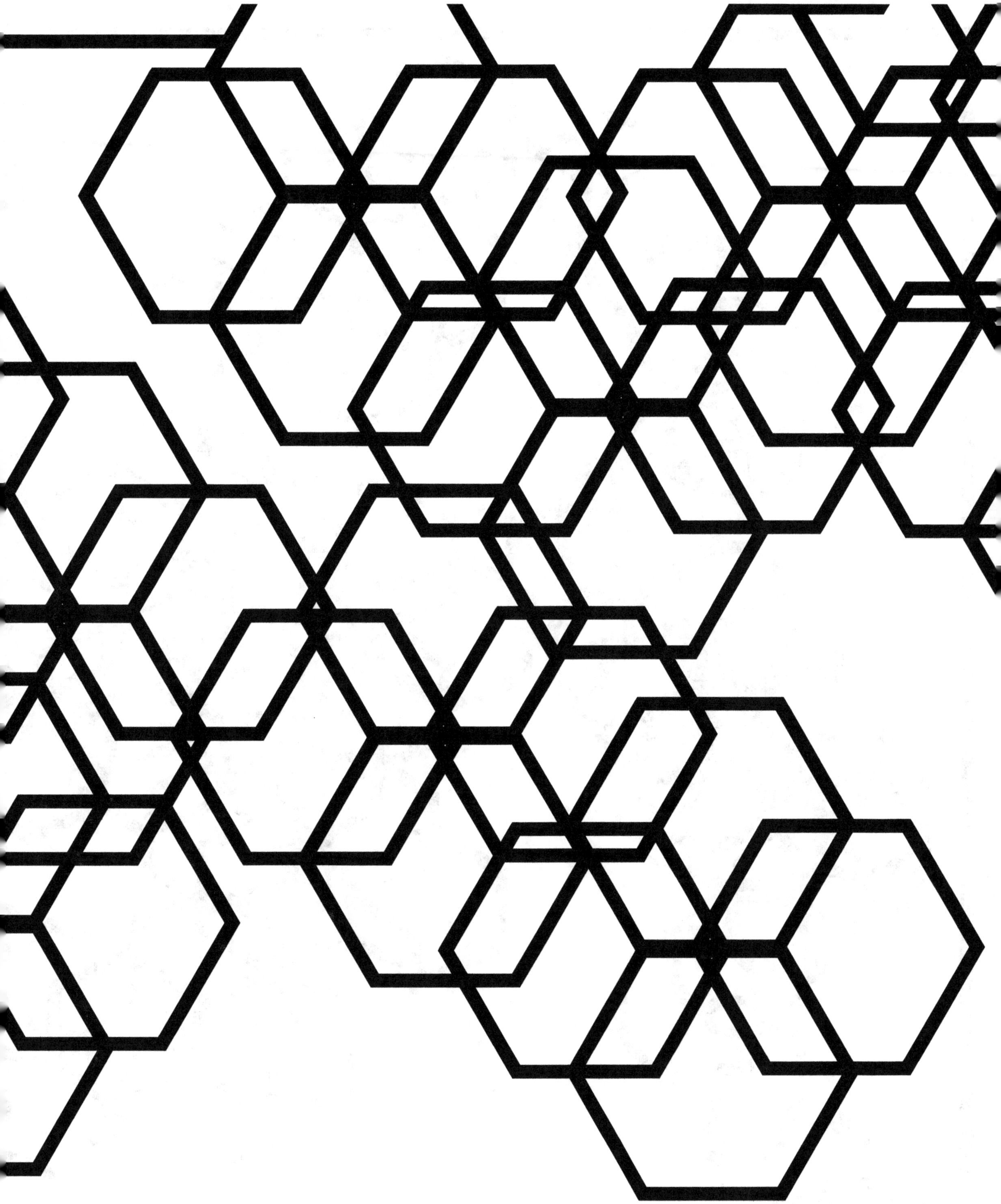

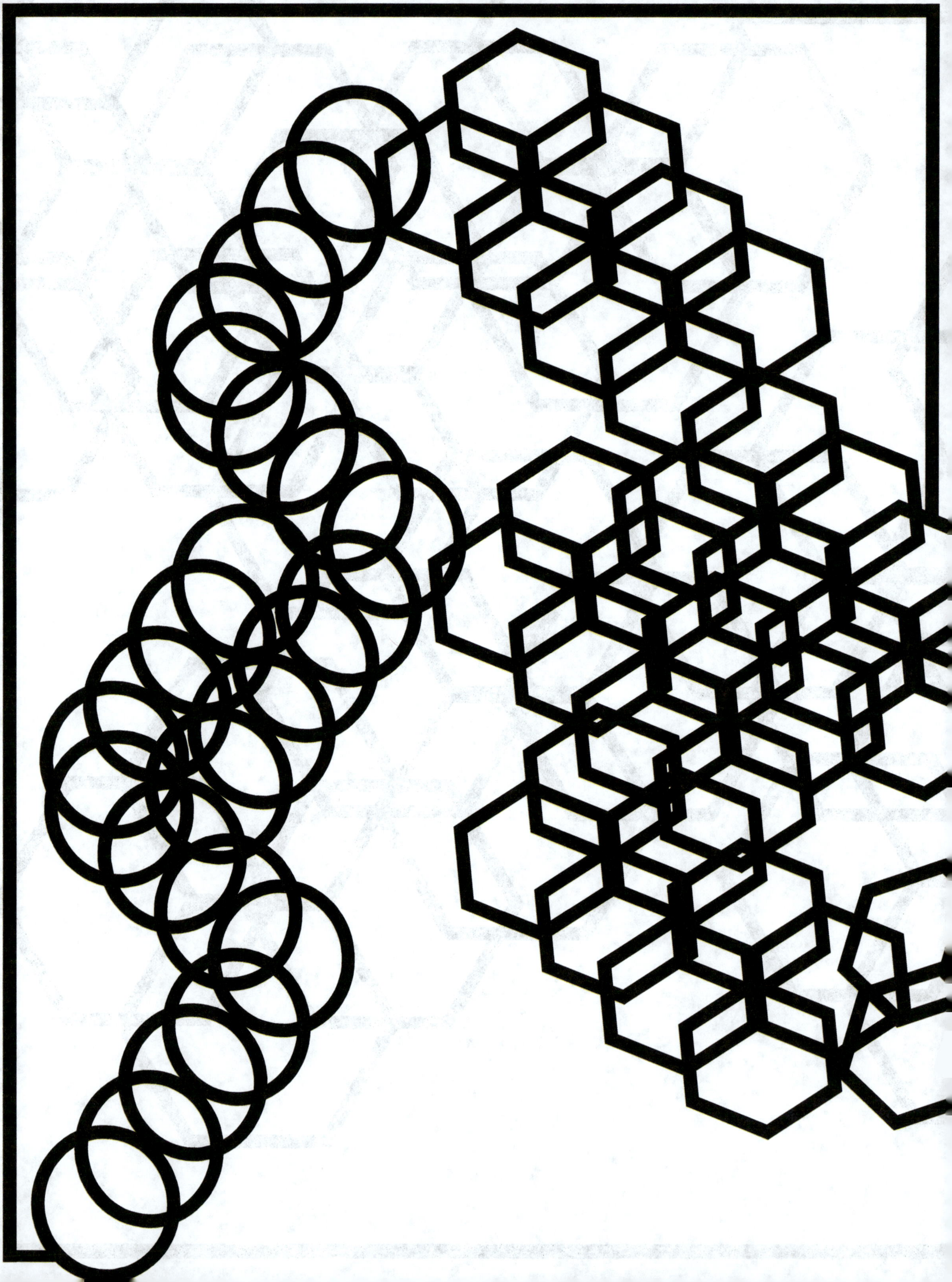

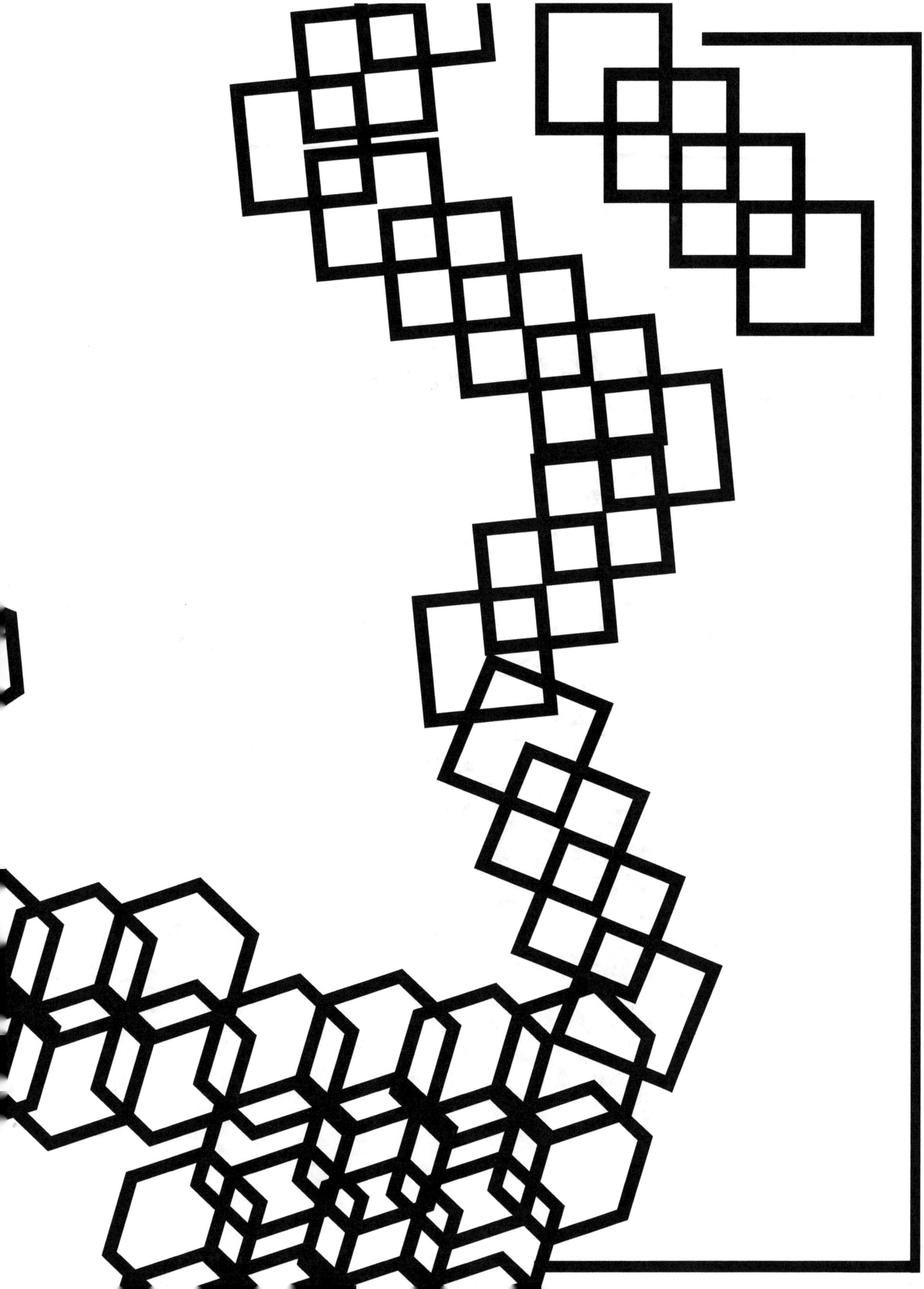

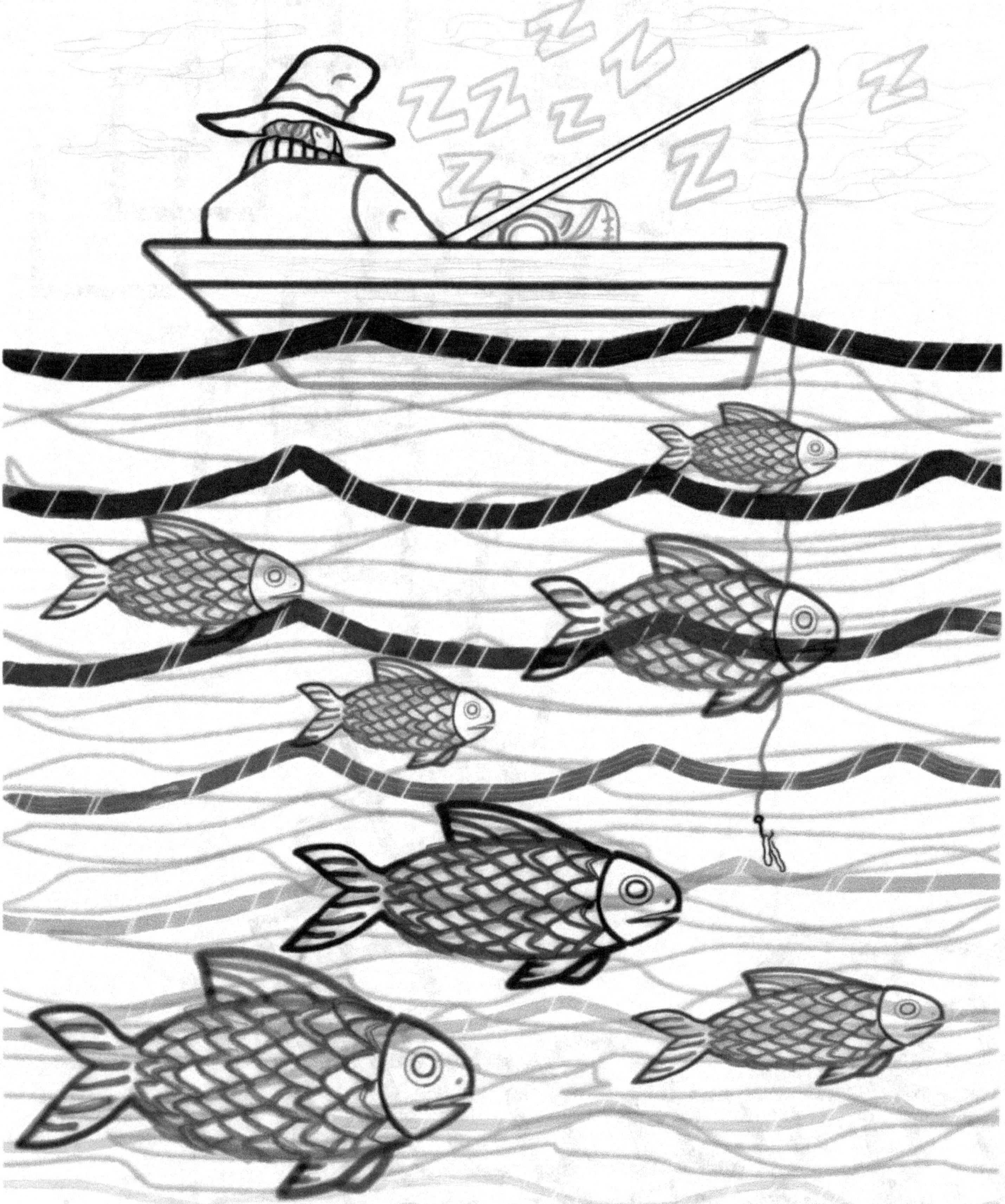

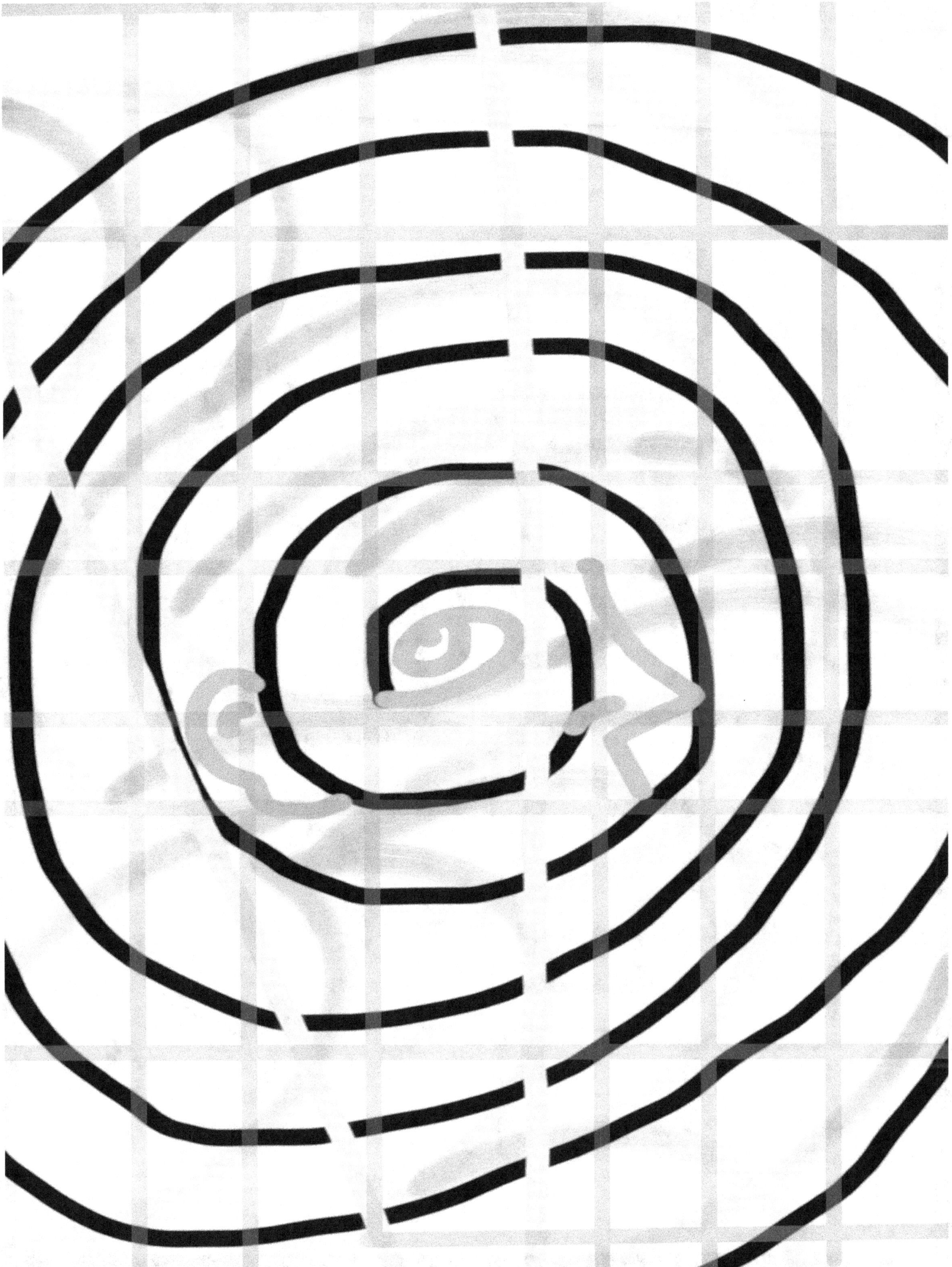

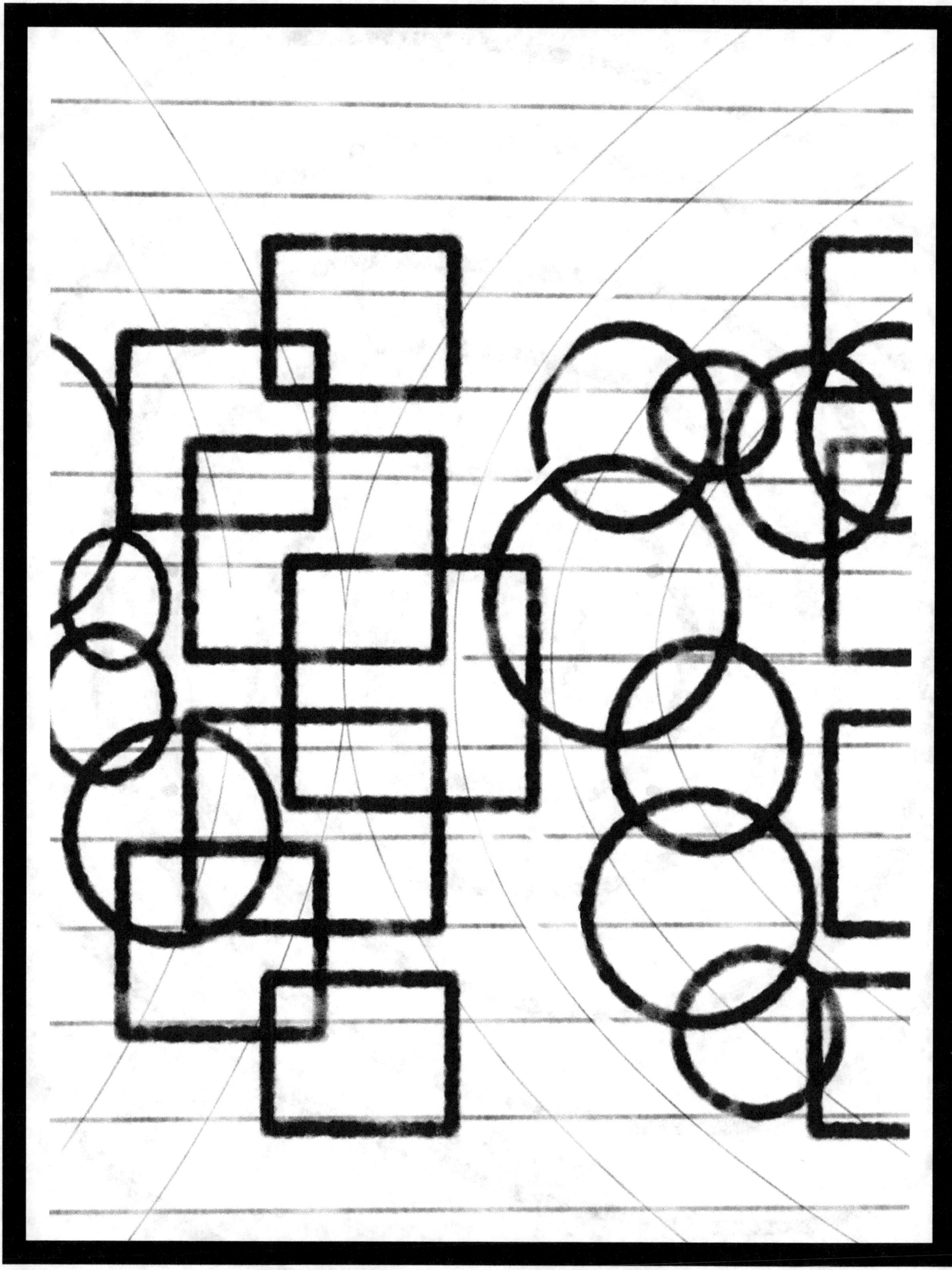

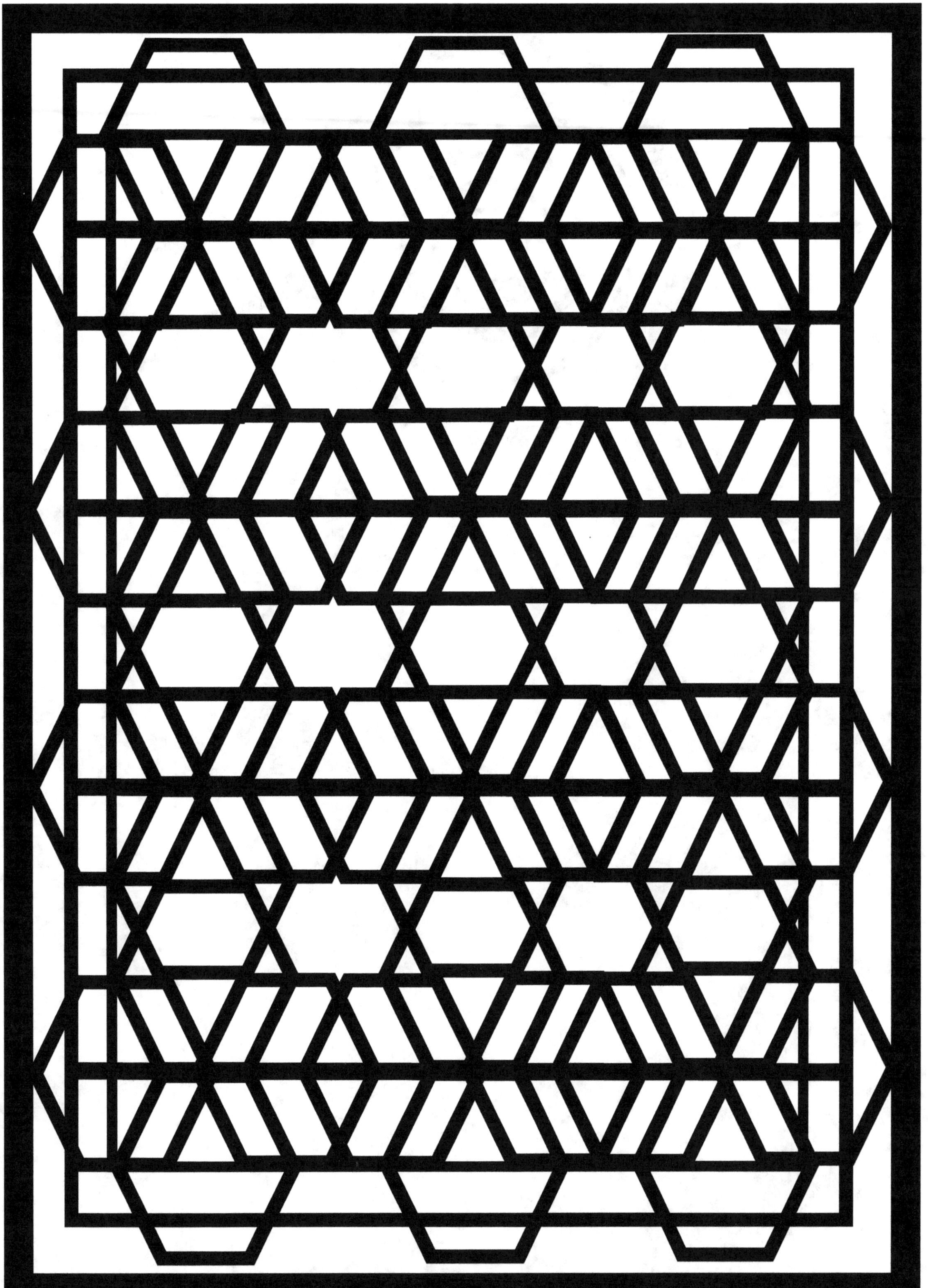

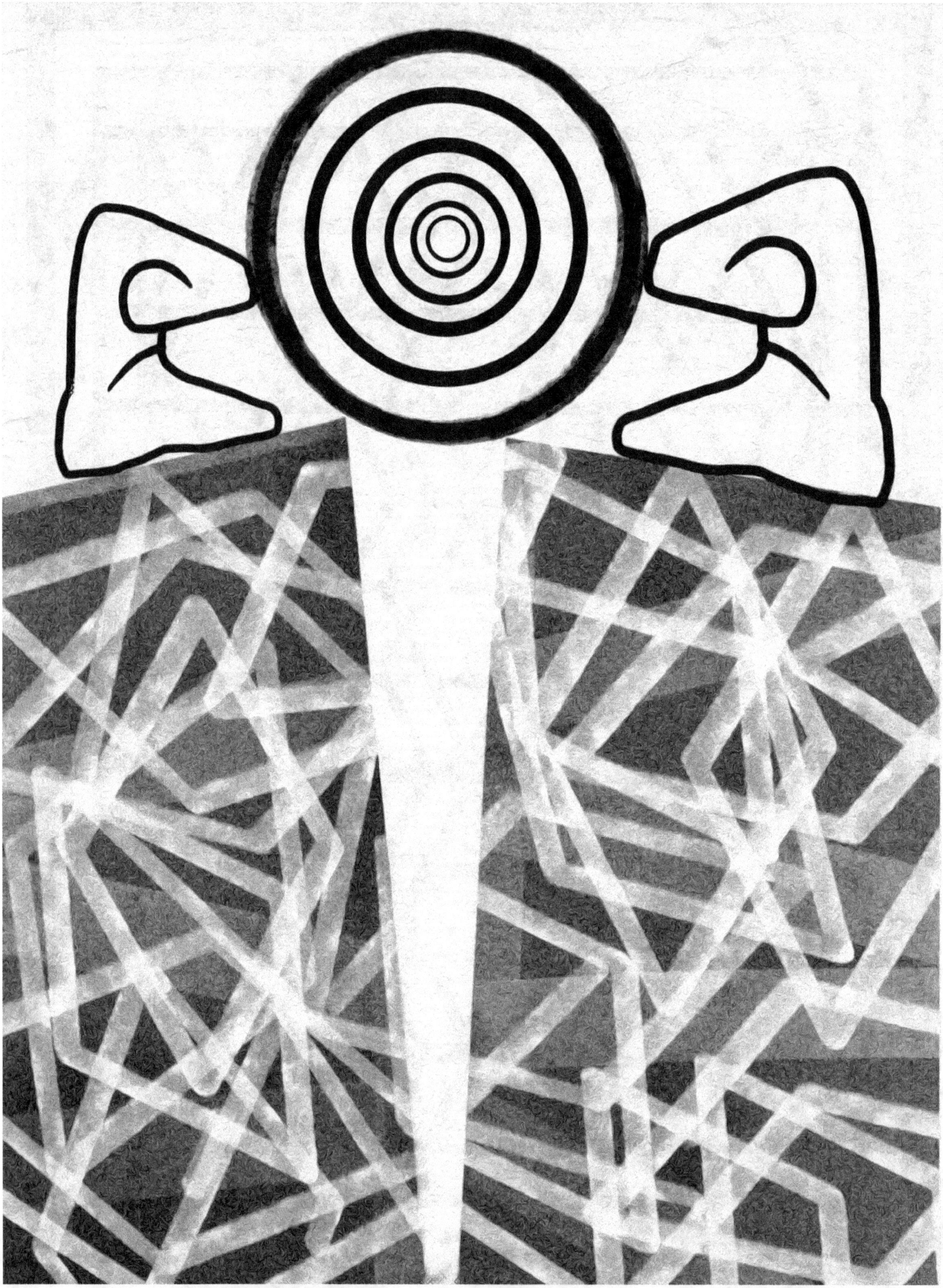

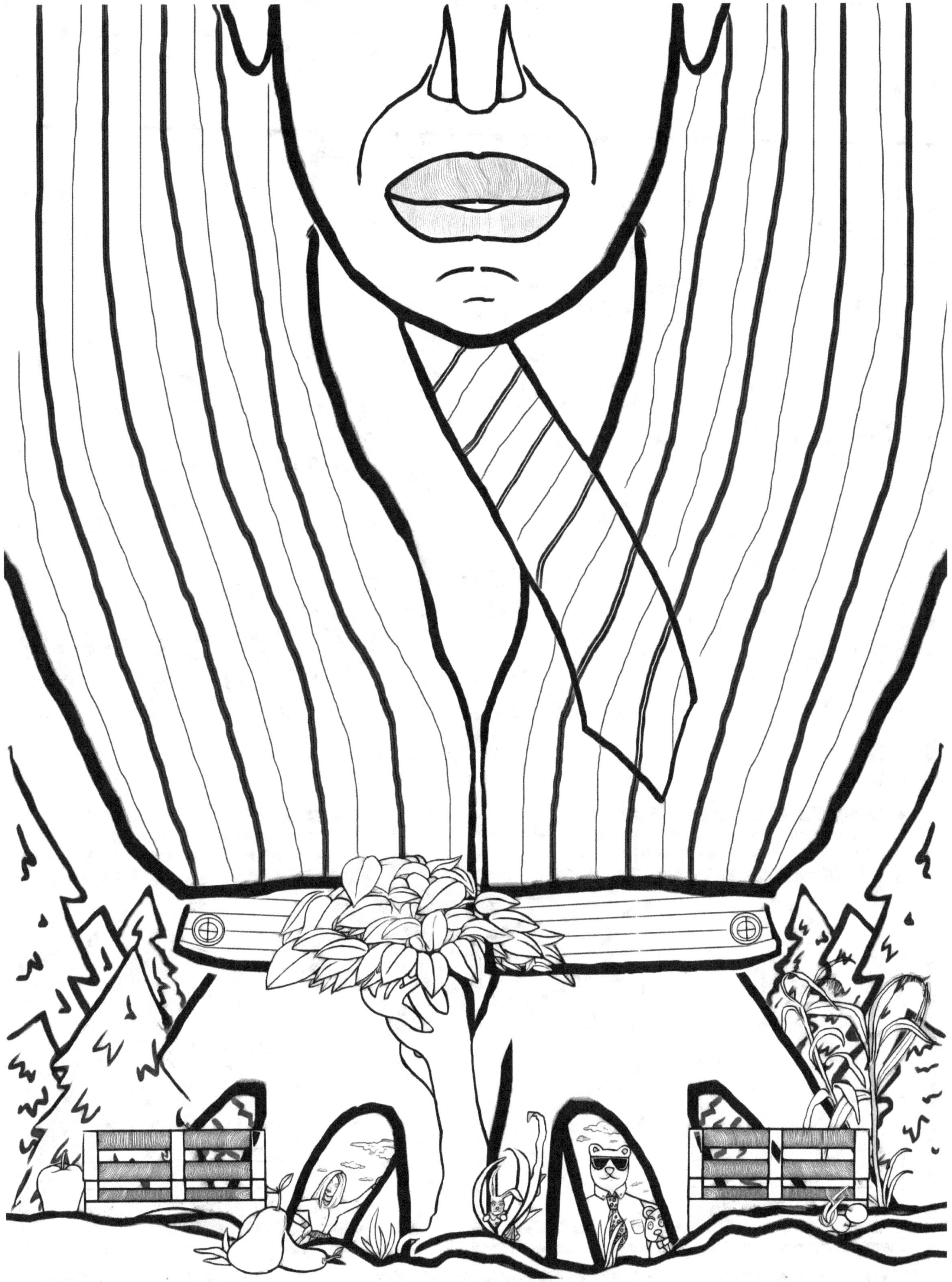

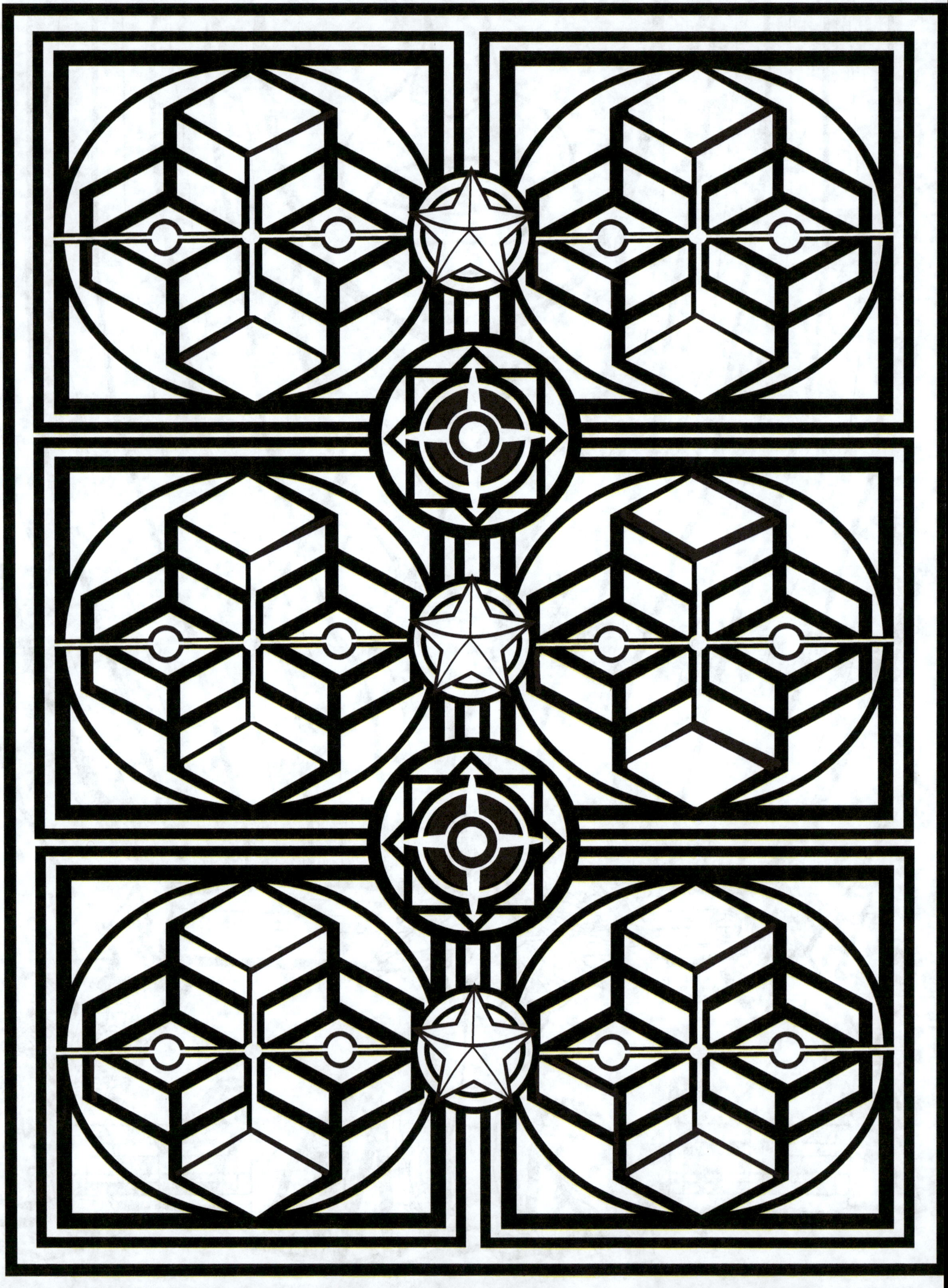

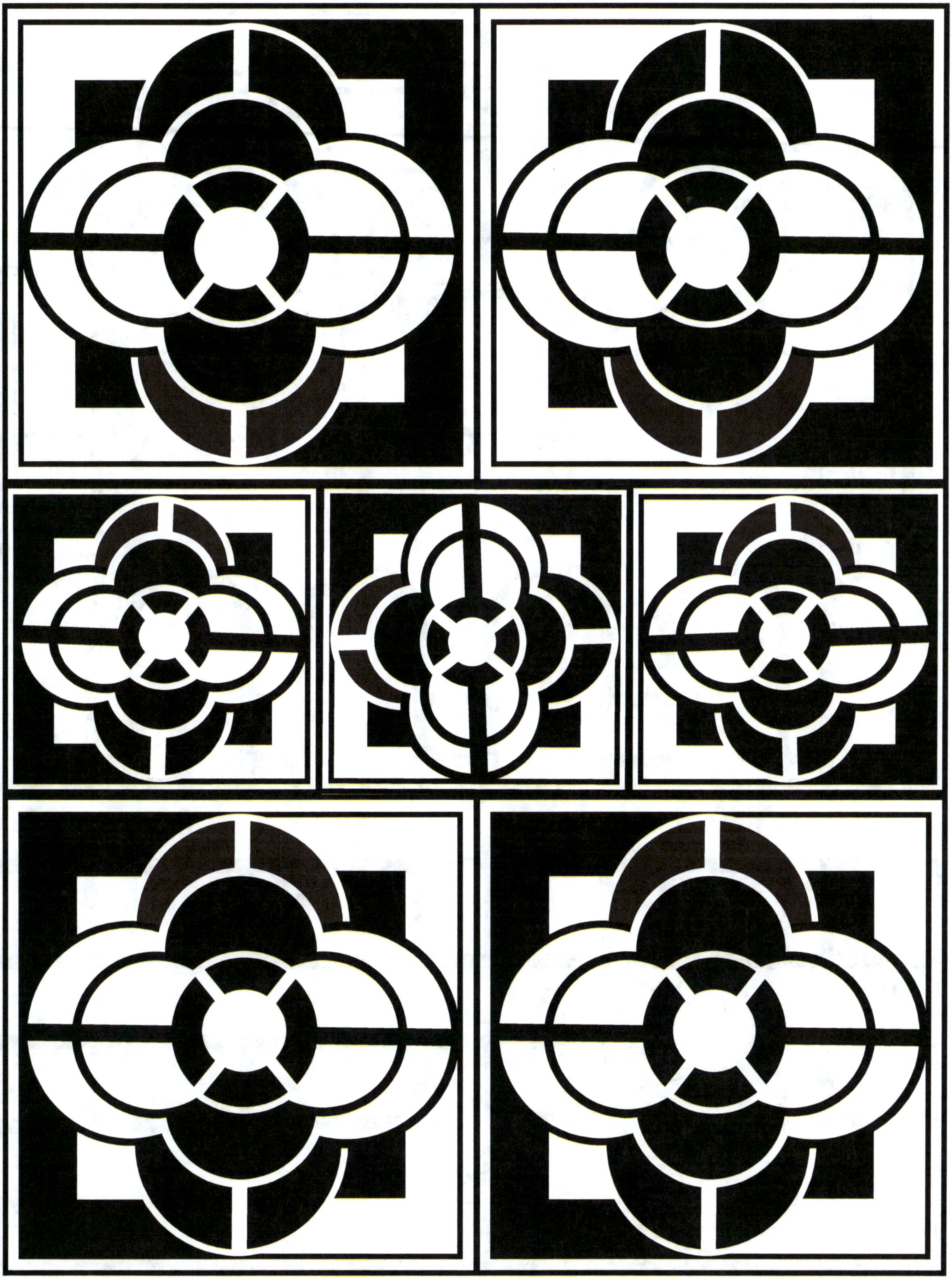

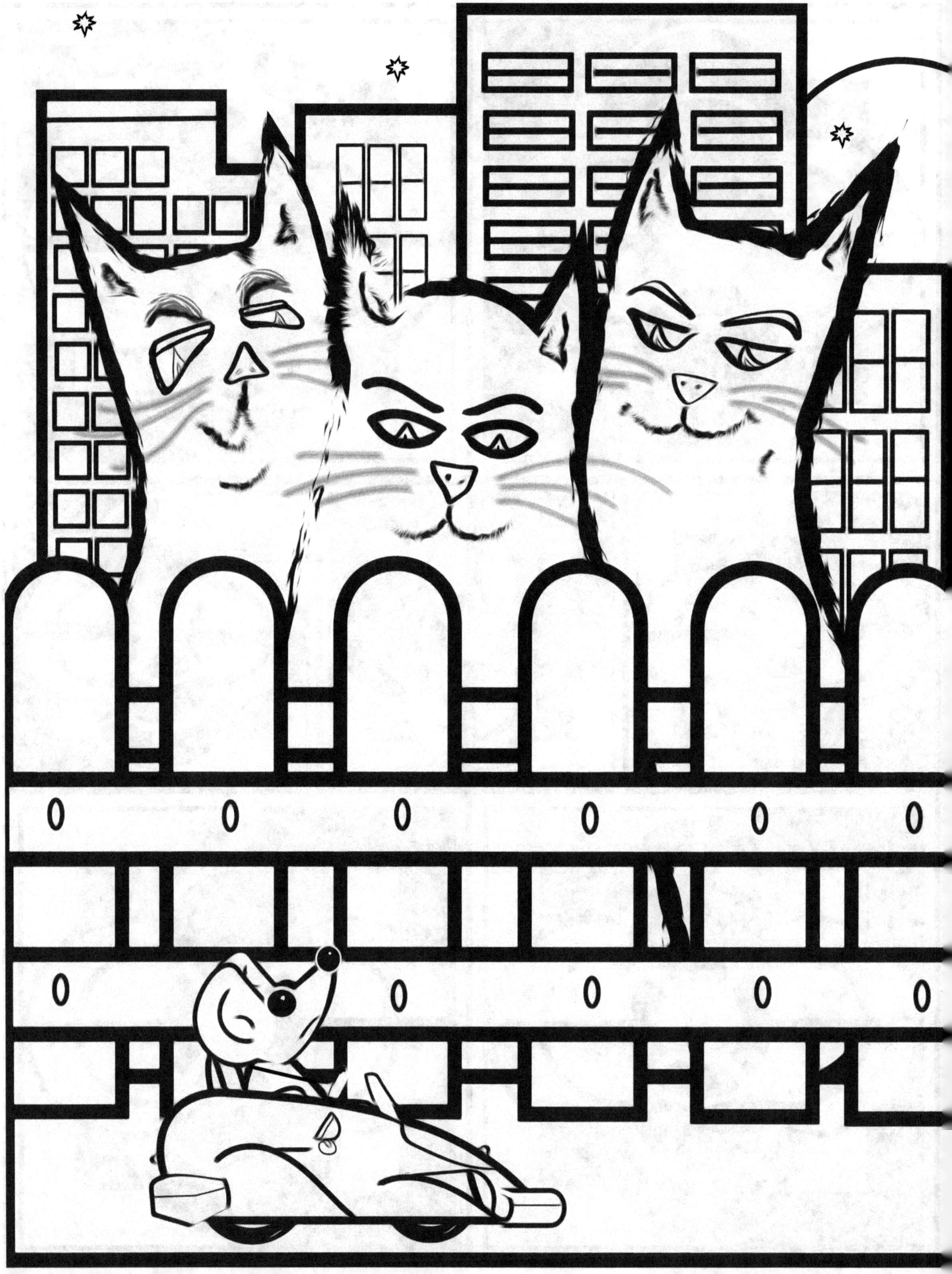

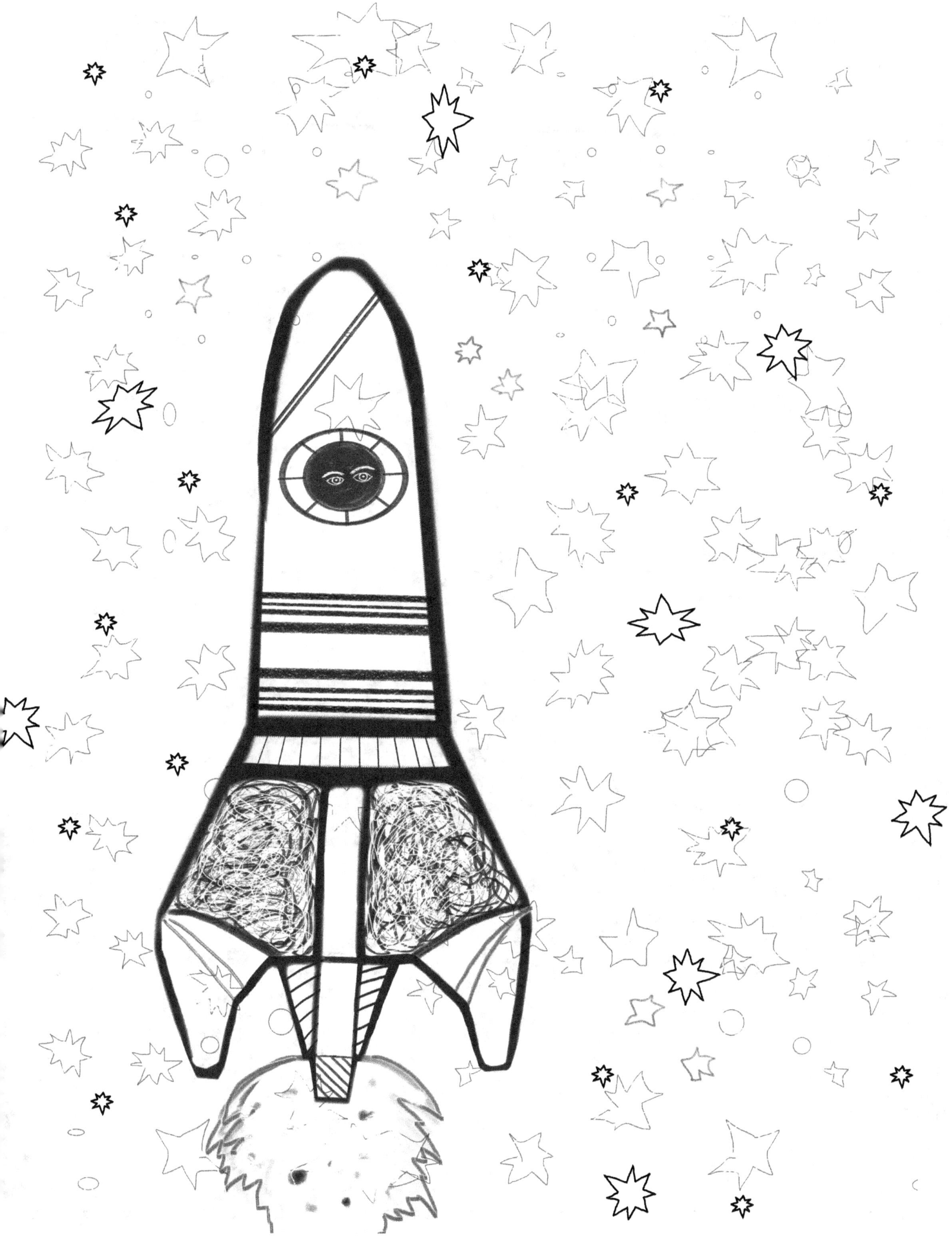

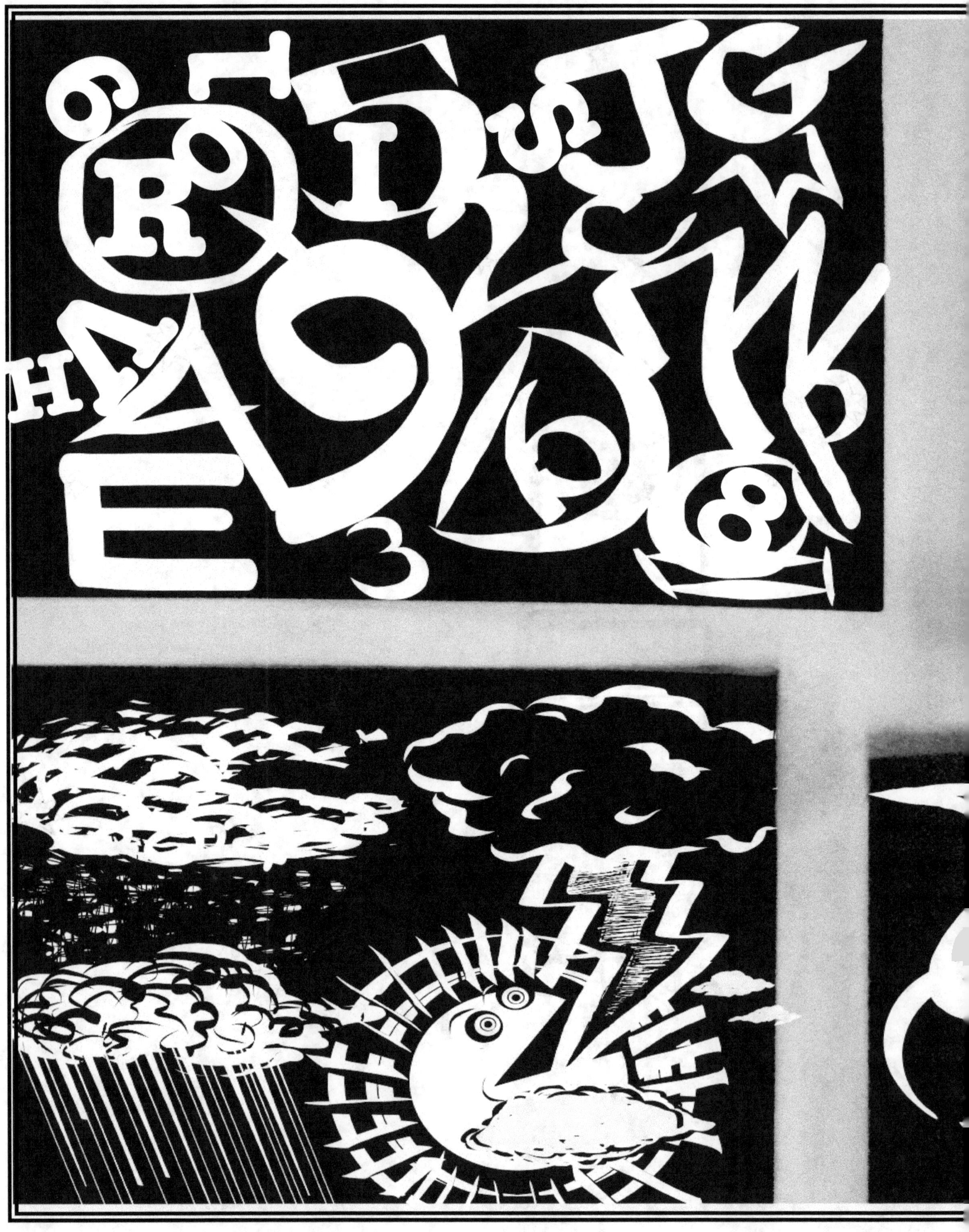

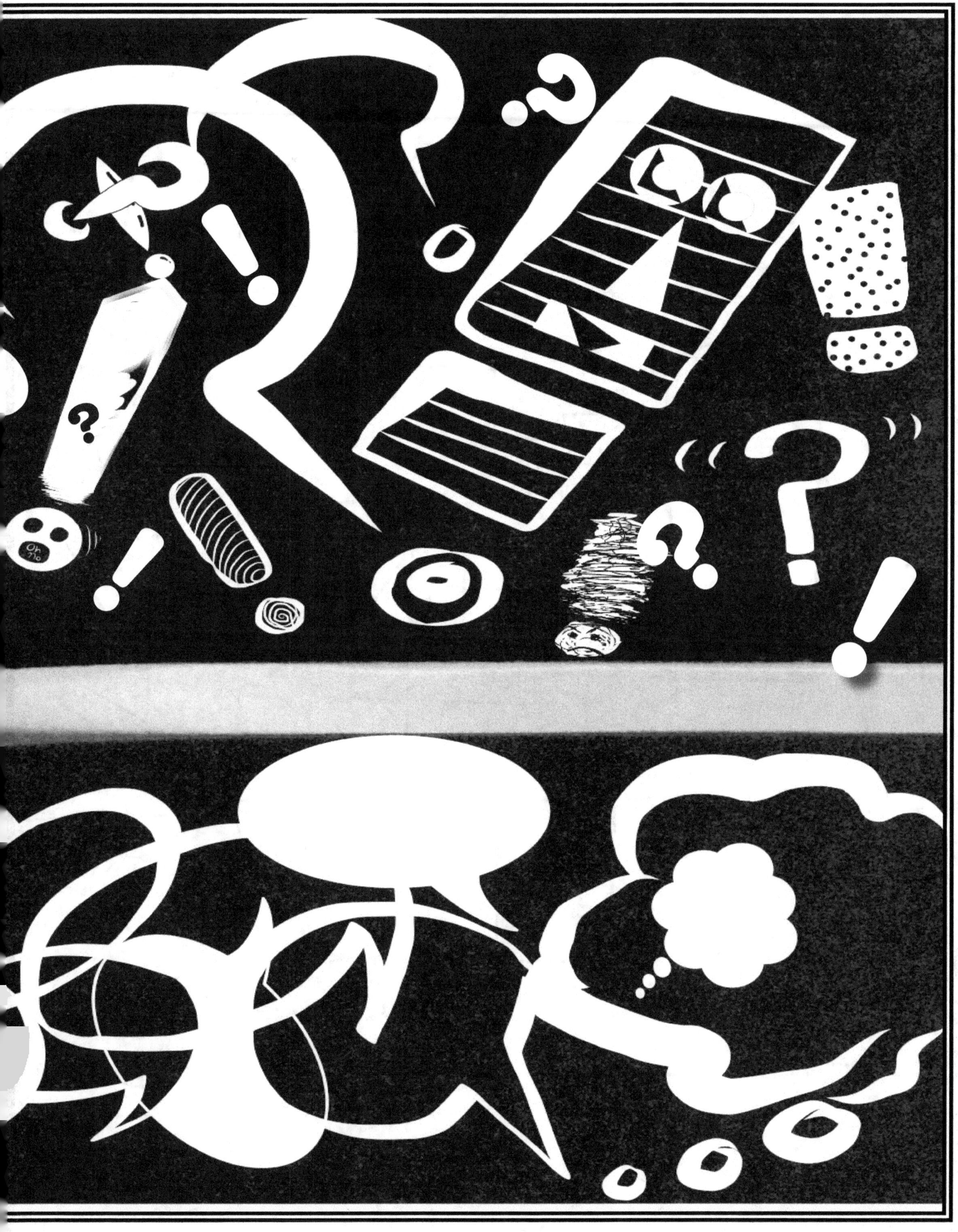
Oh no

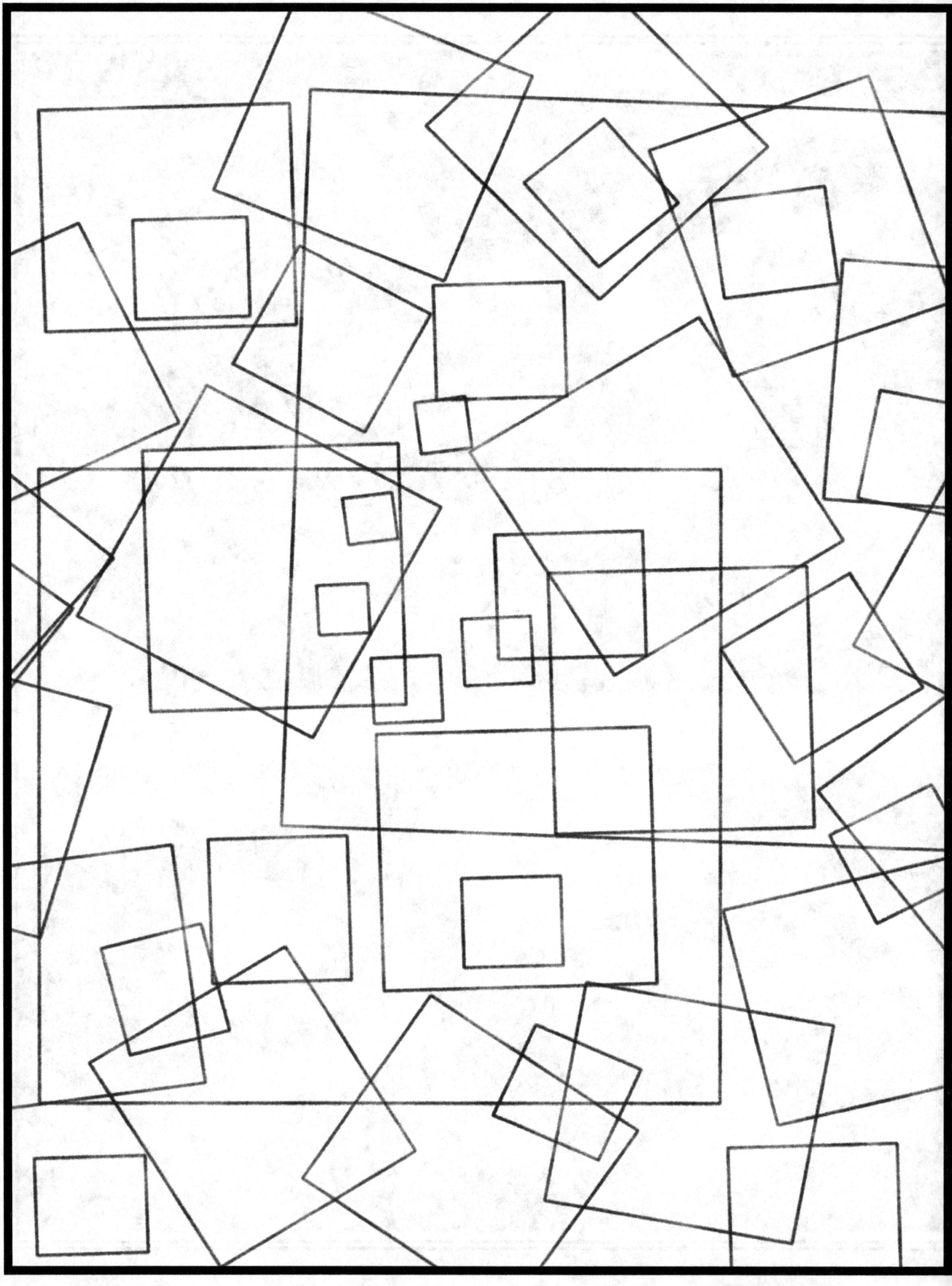

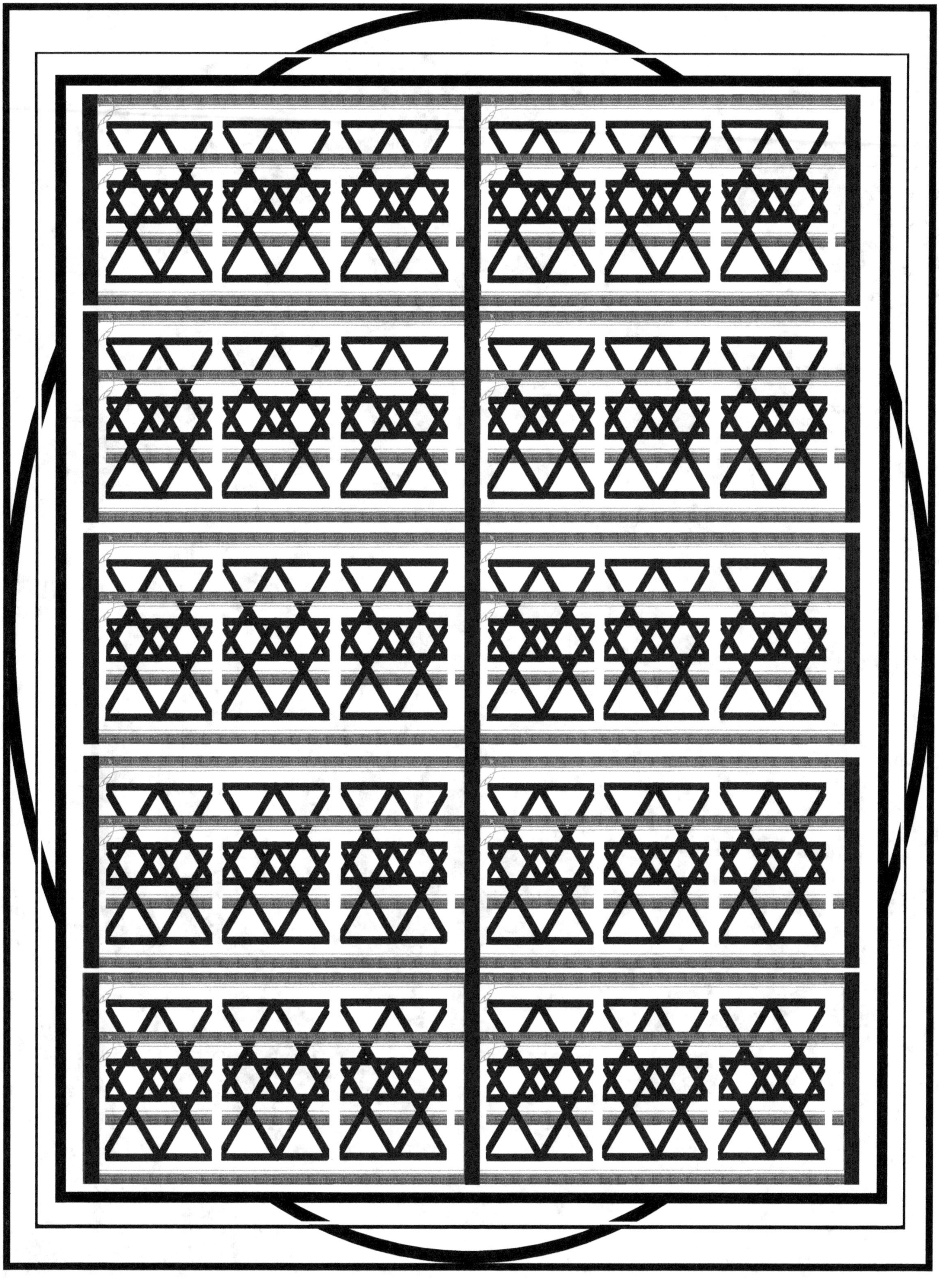

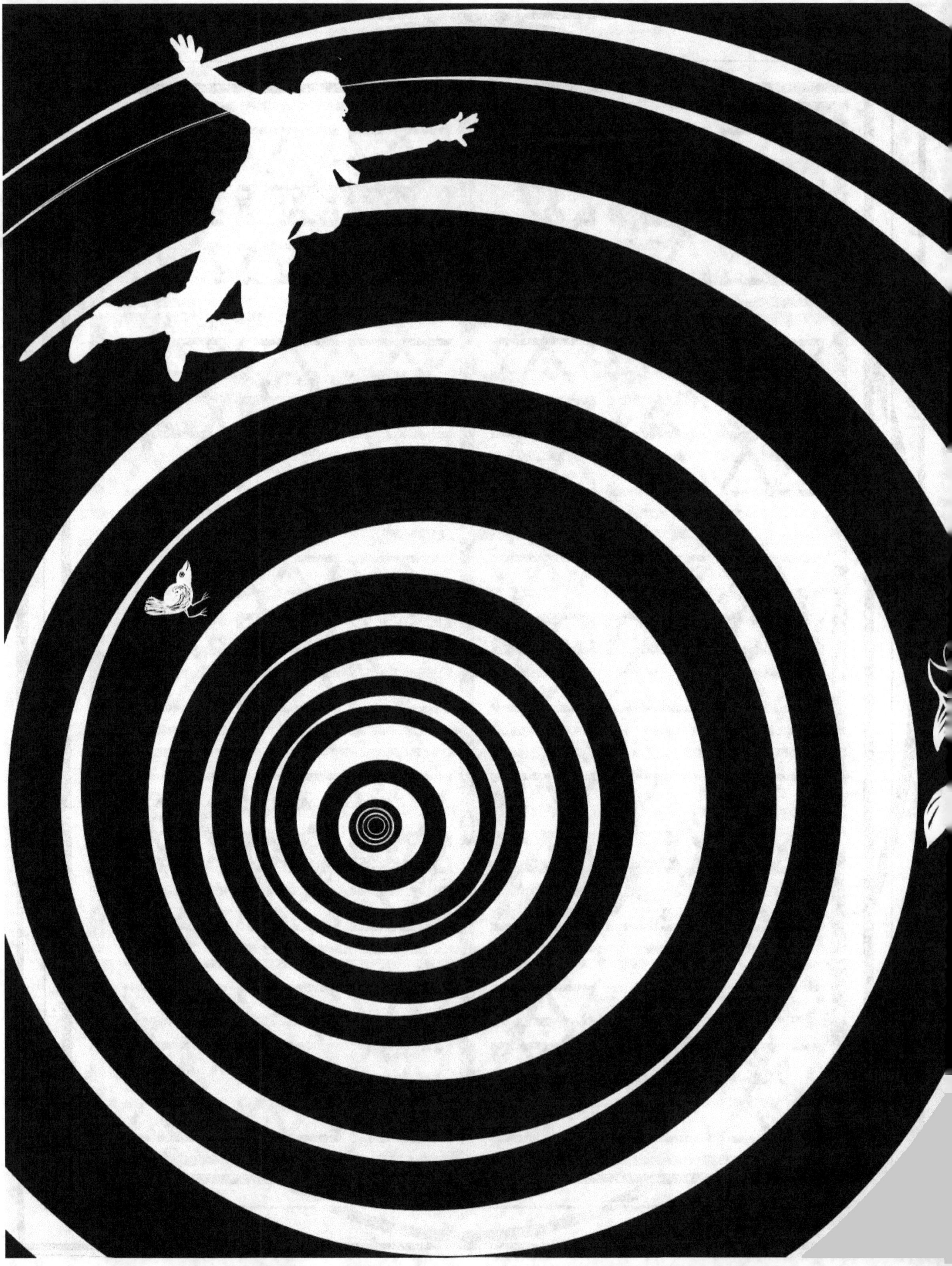

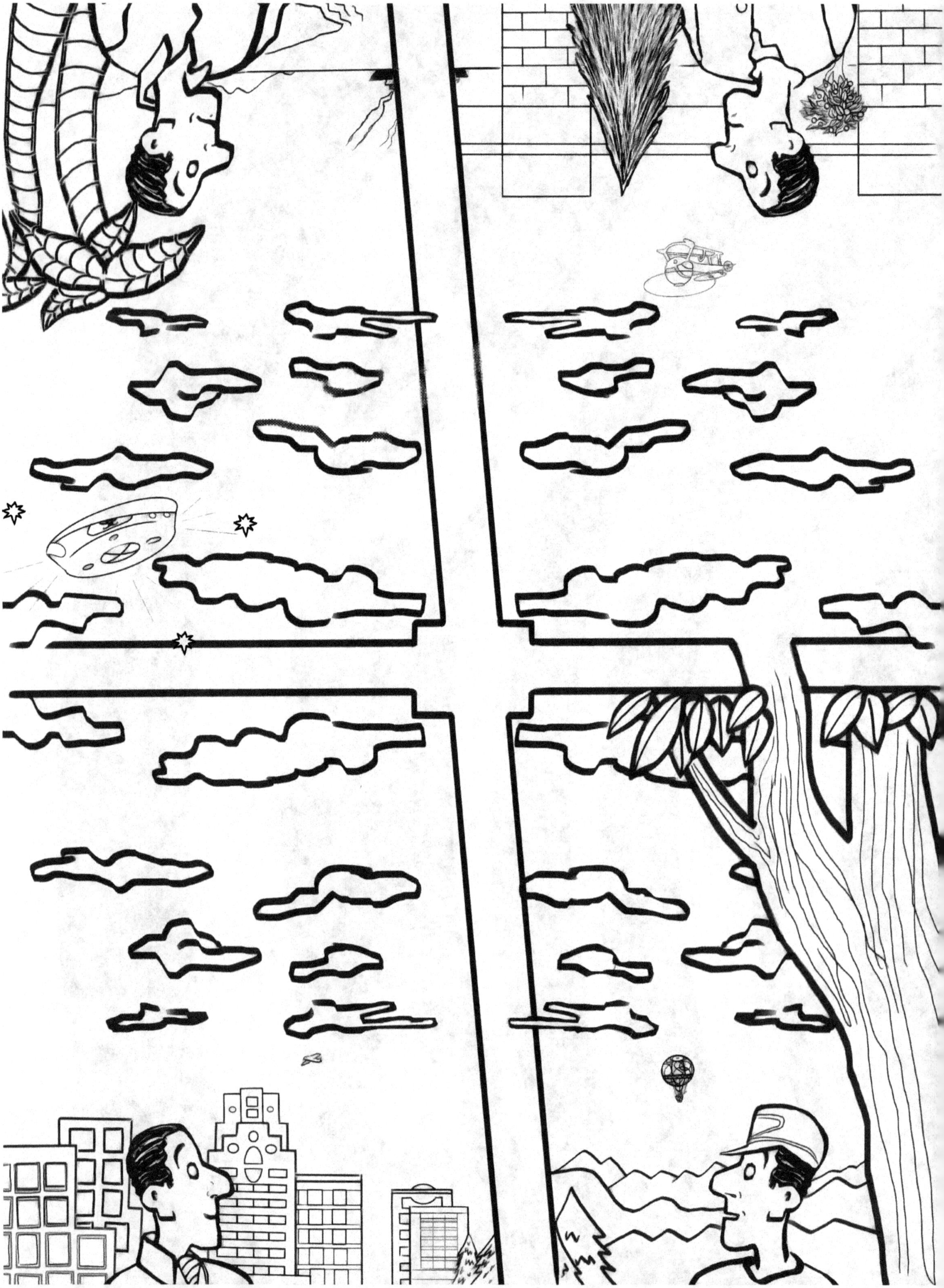

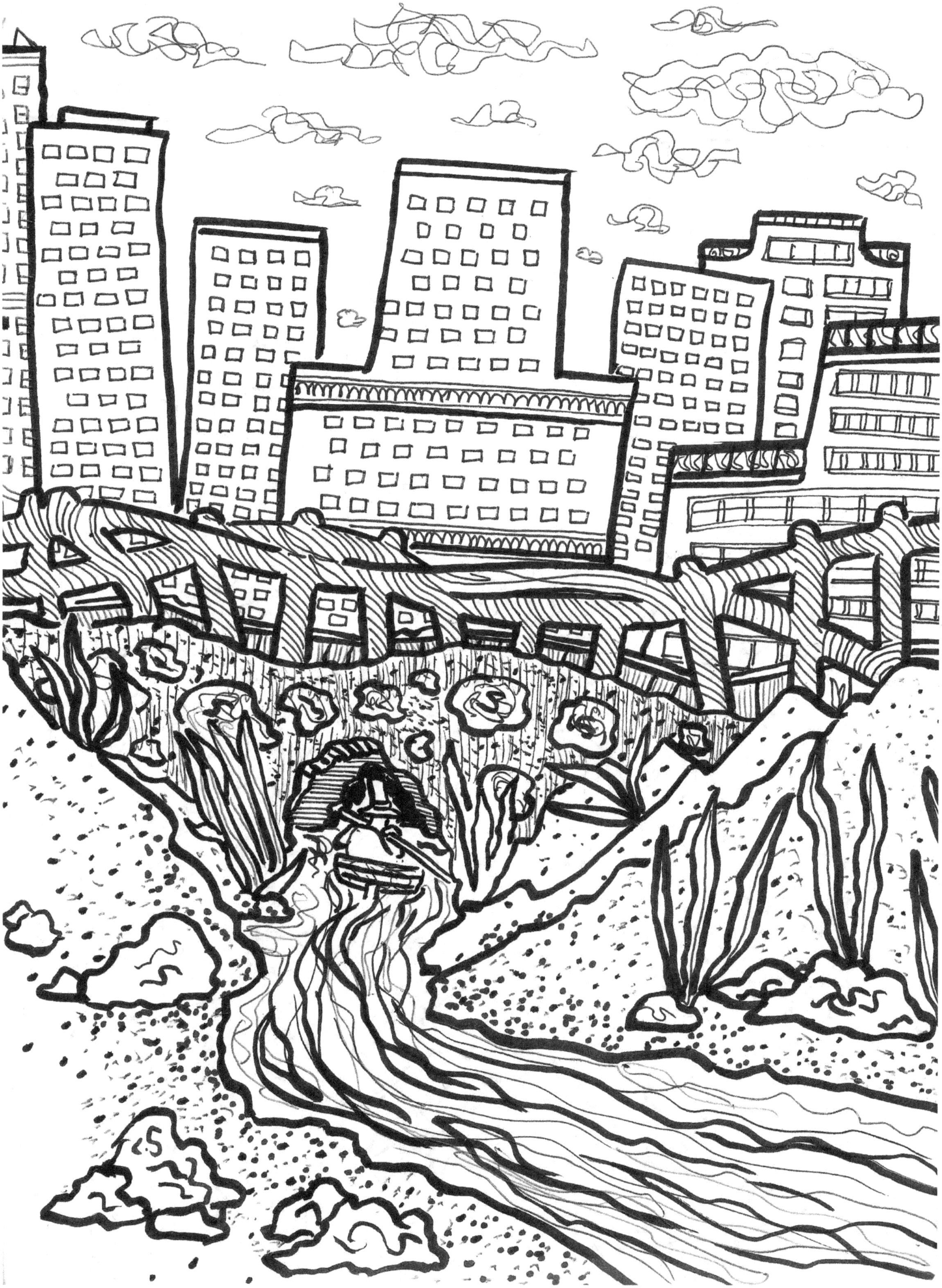

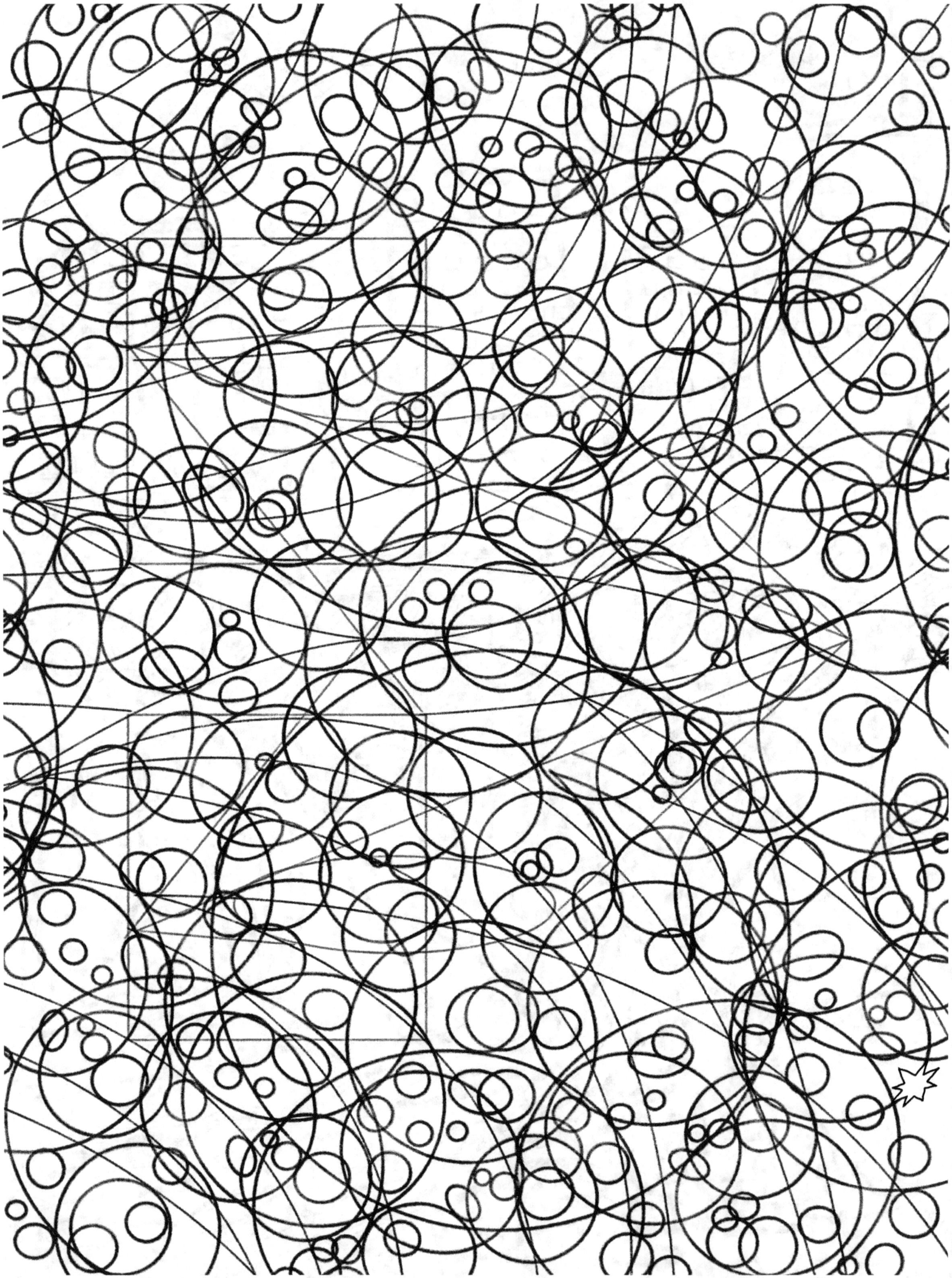

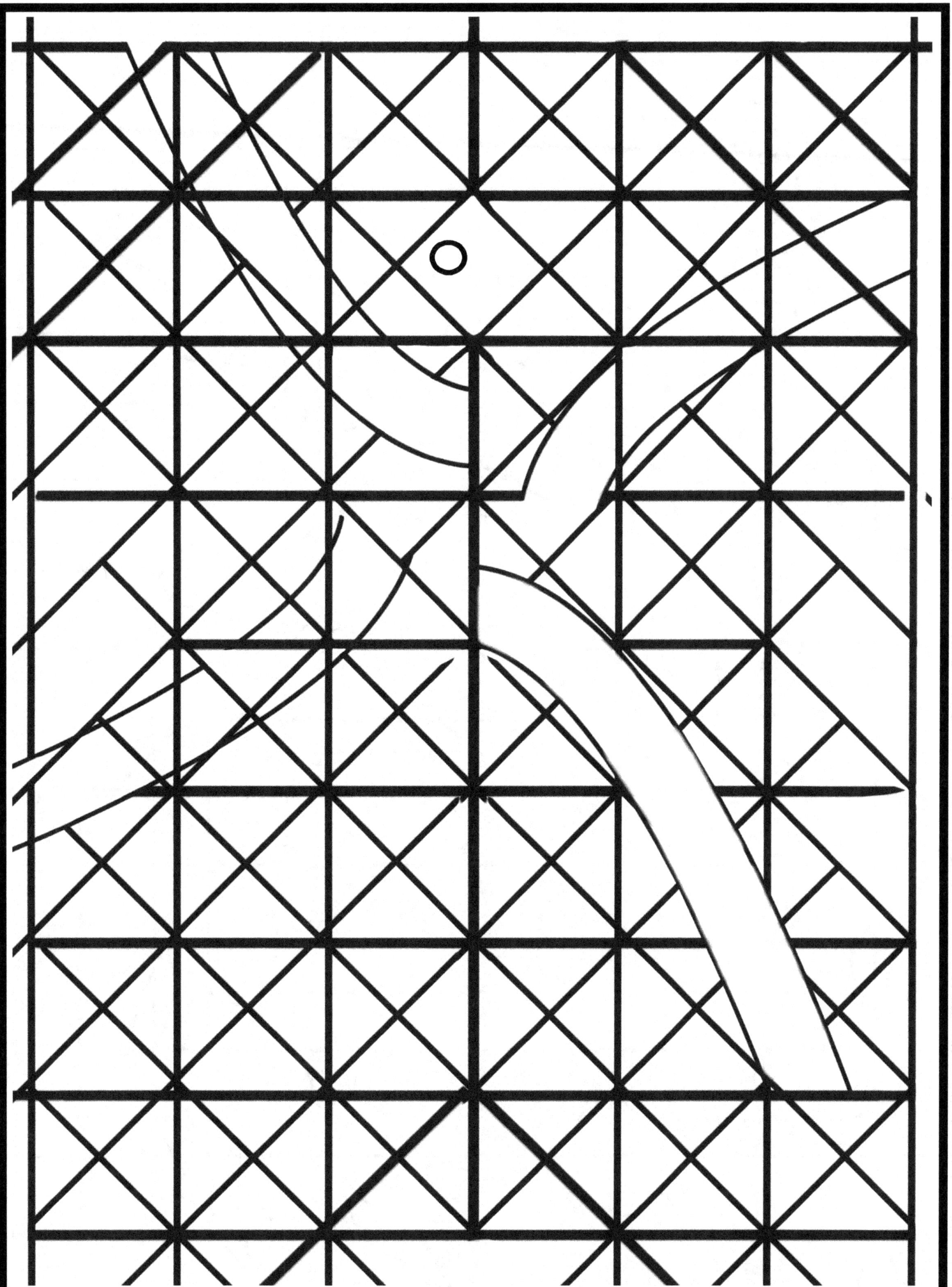

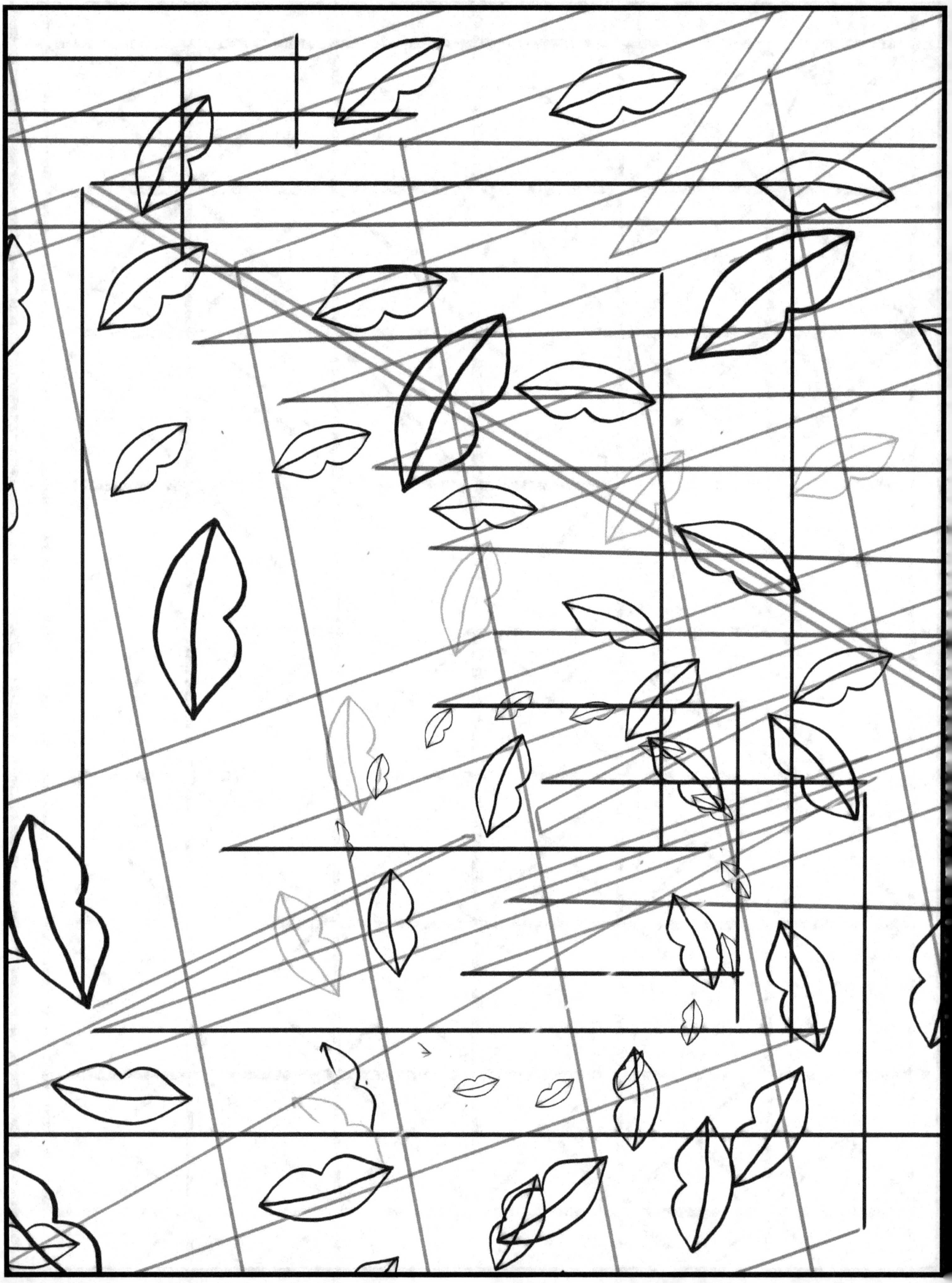

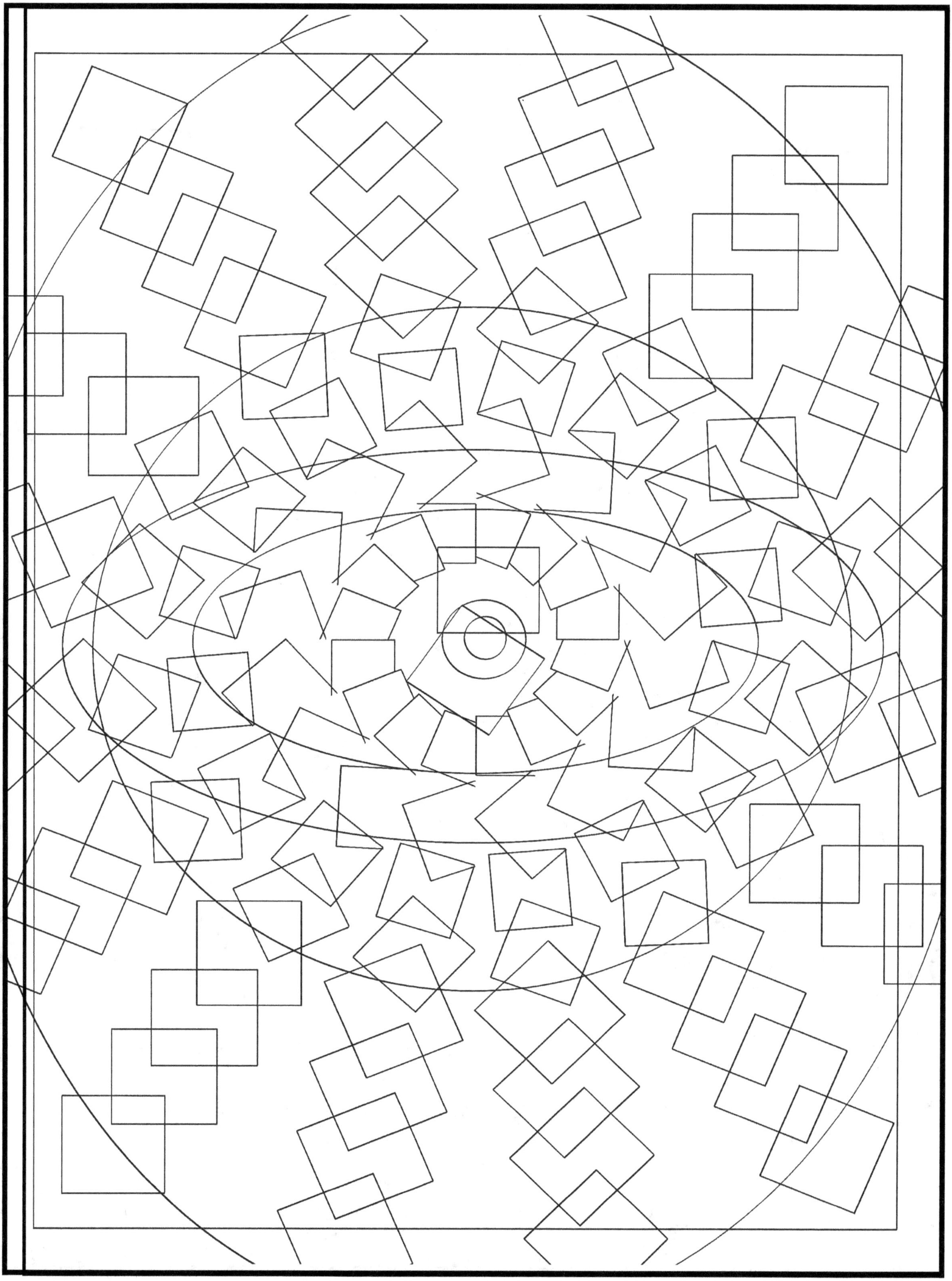

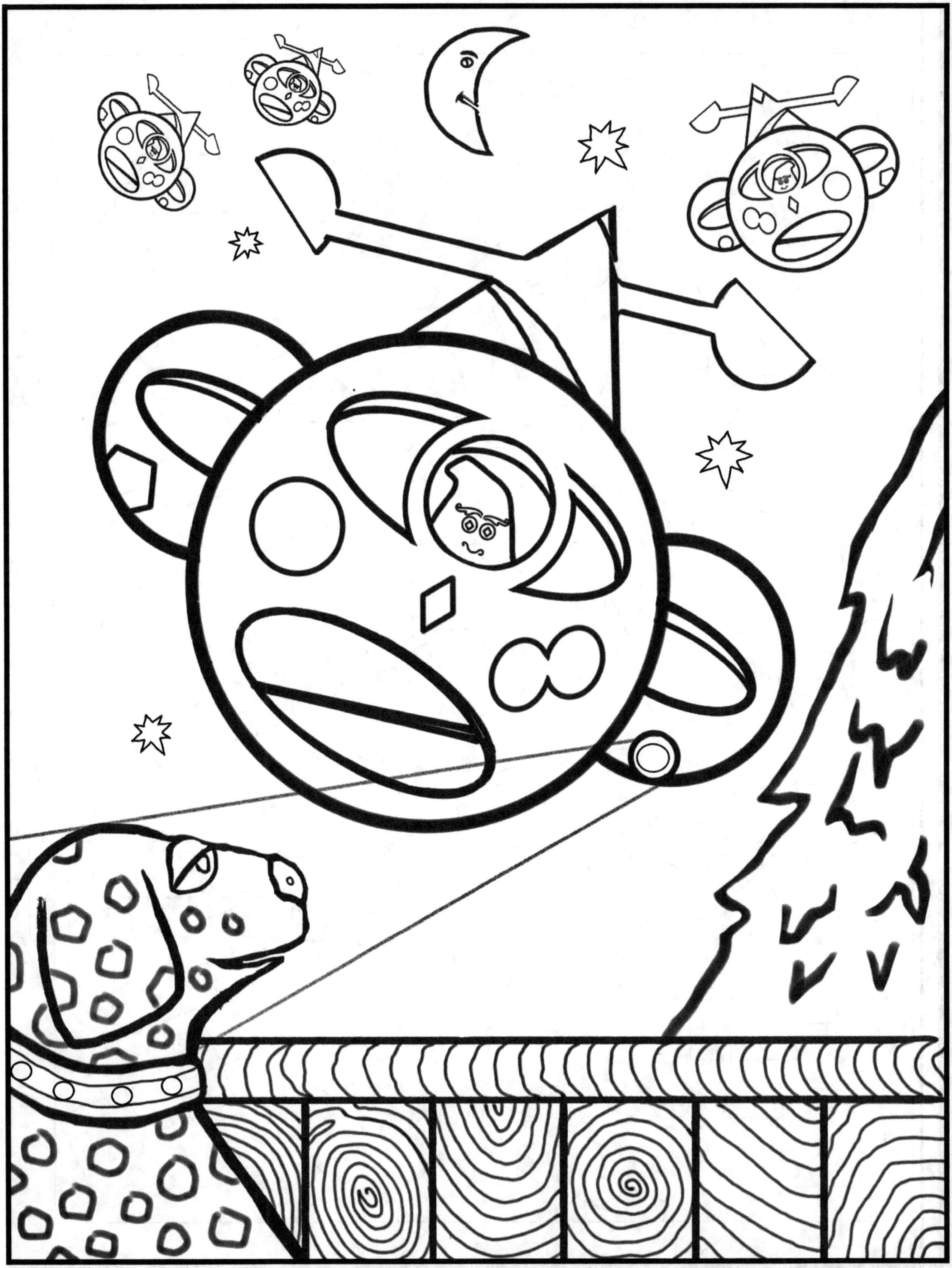

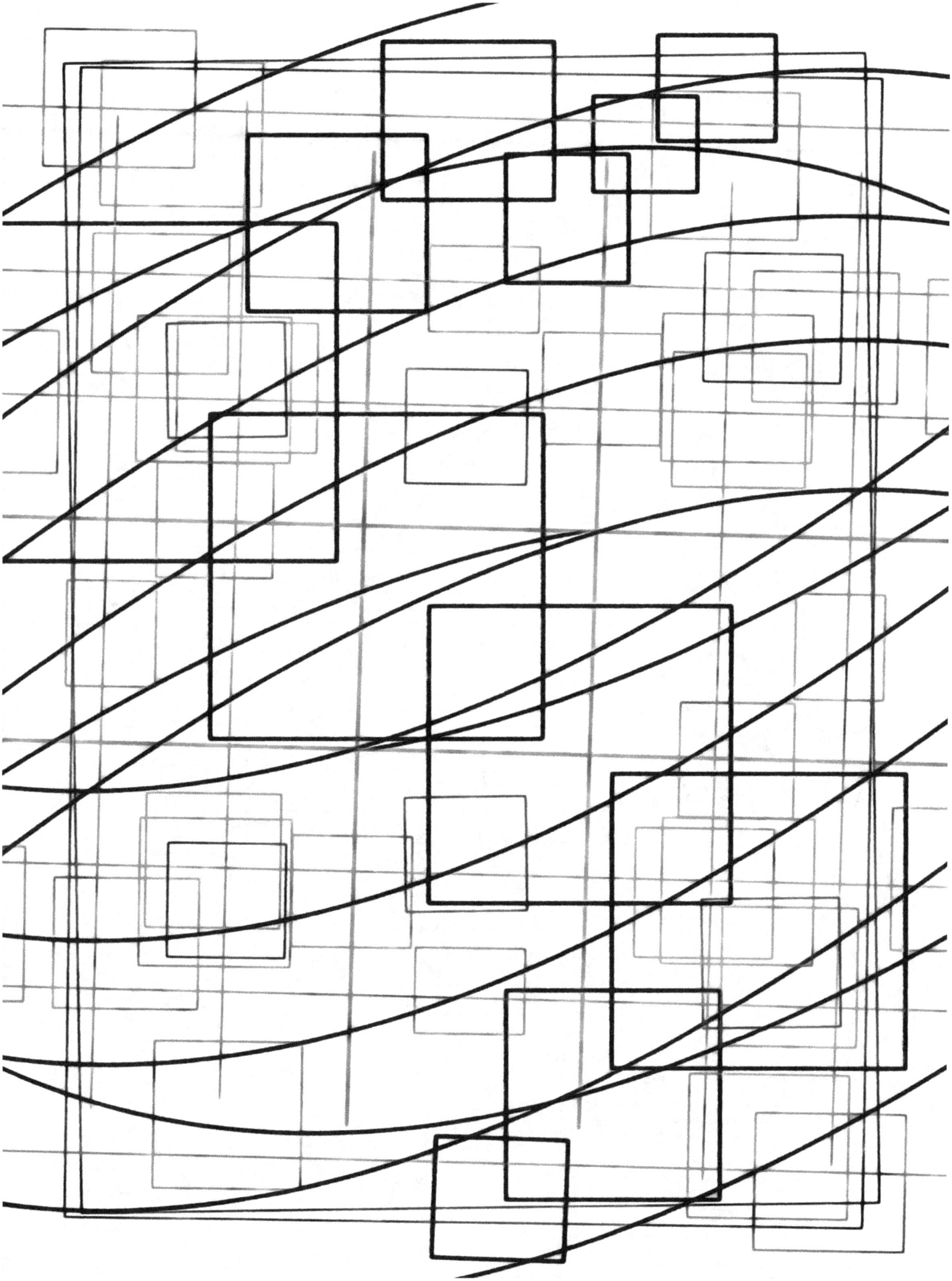

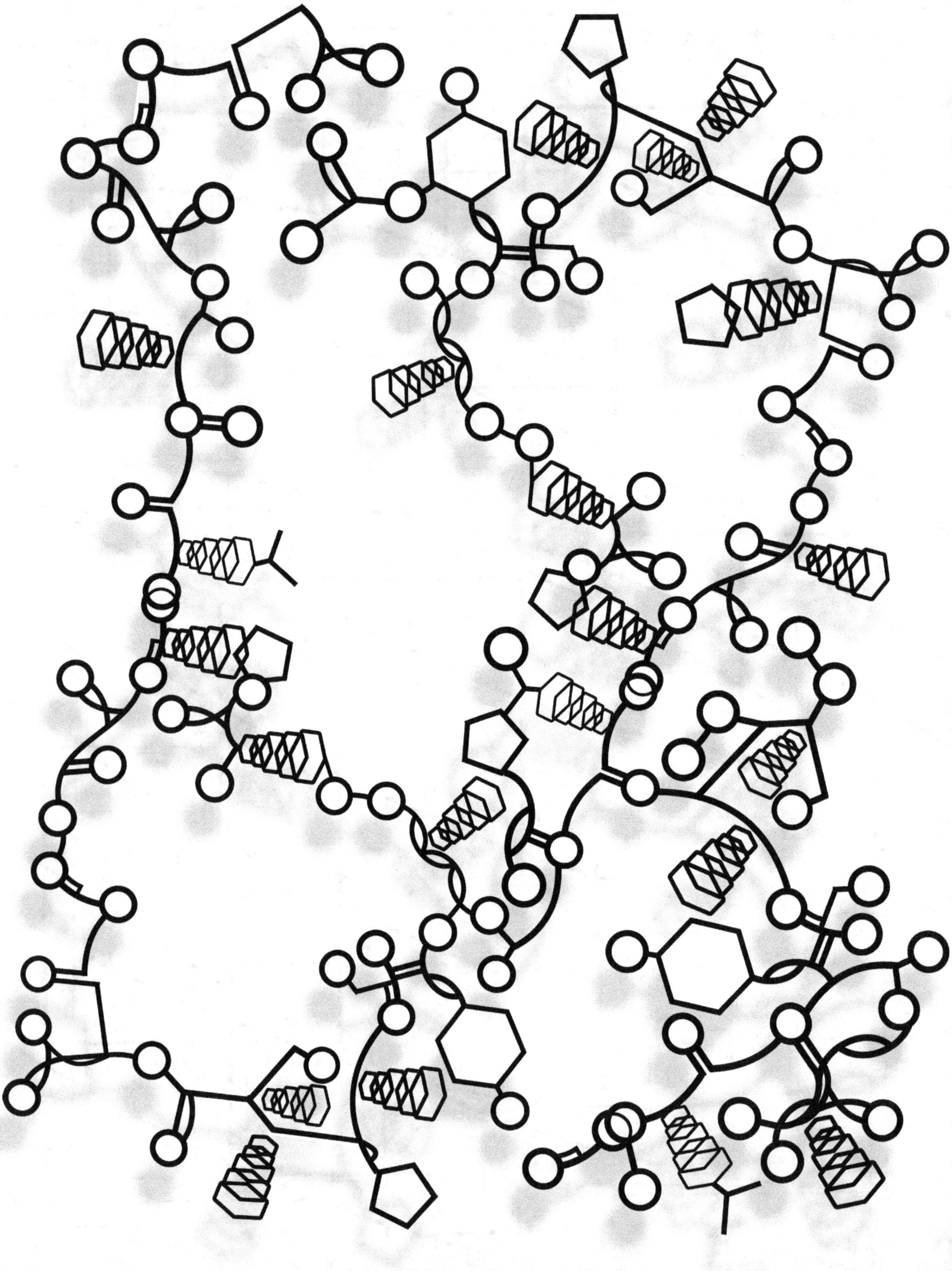

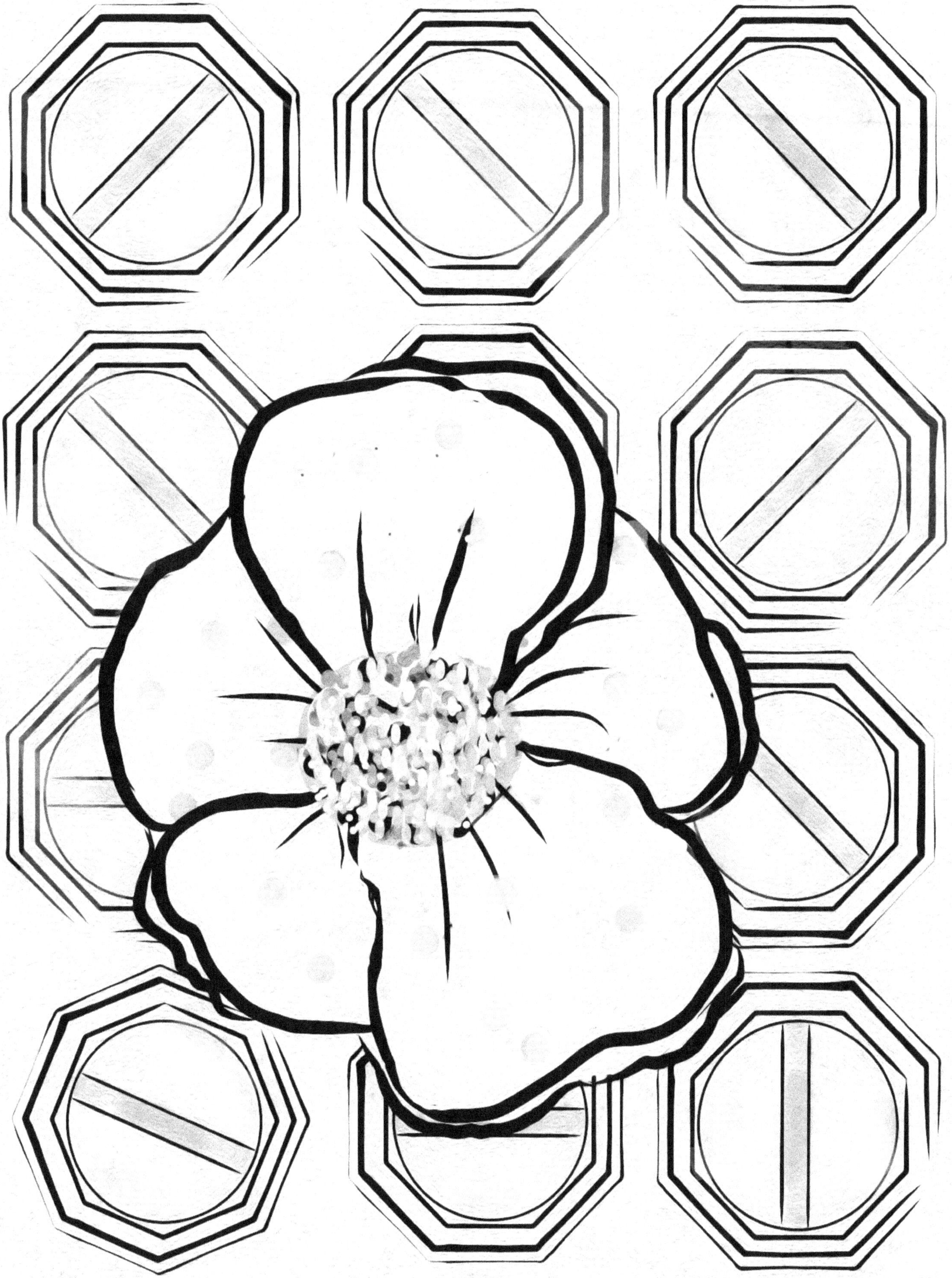

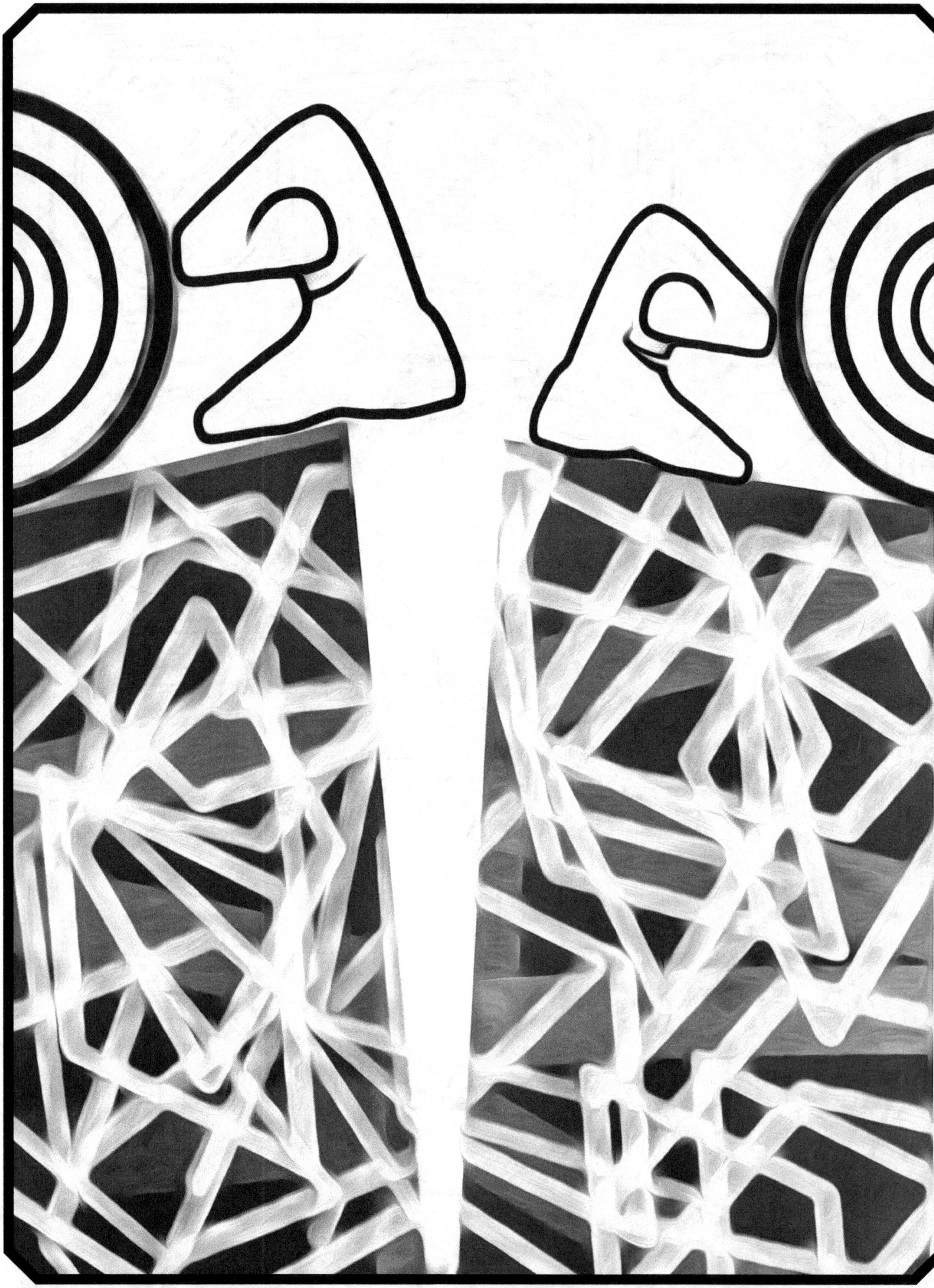

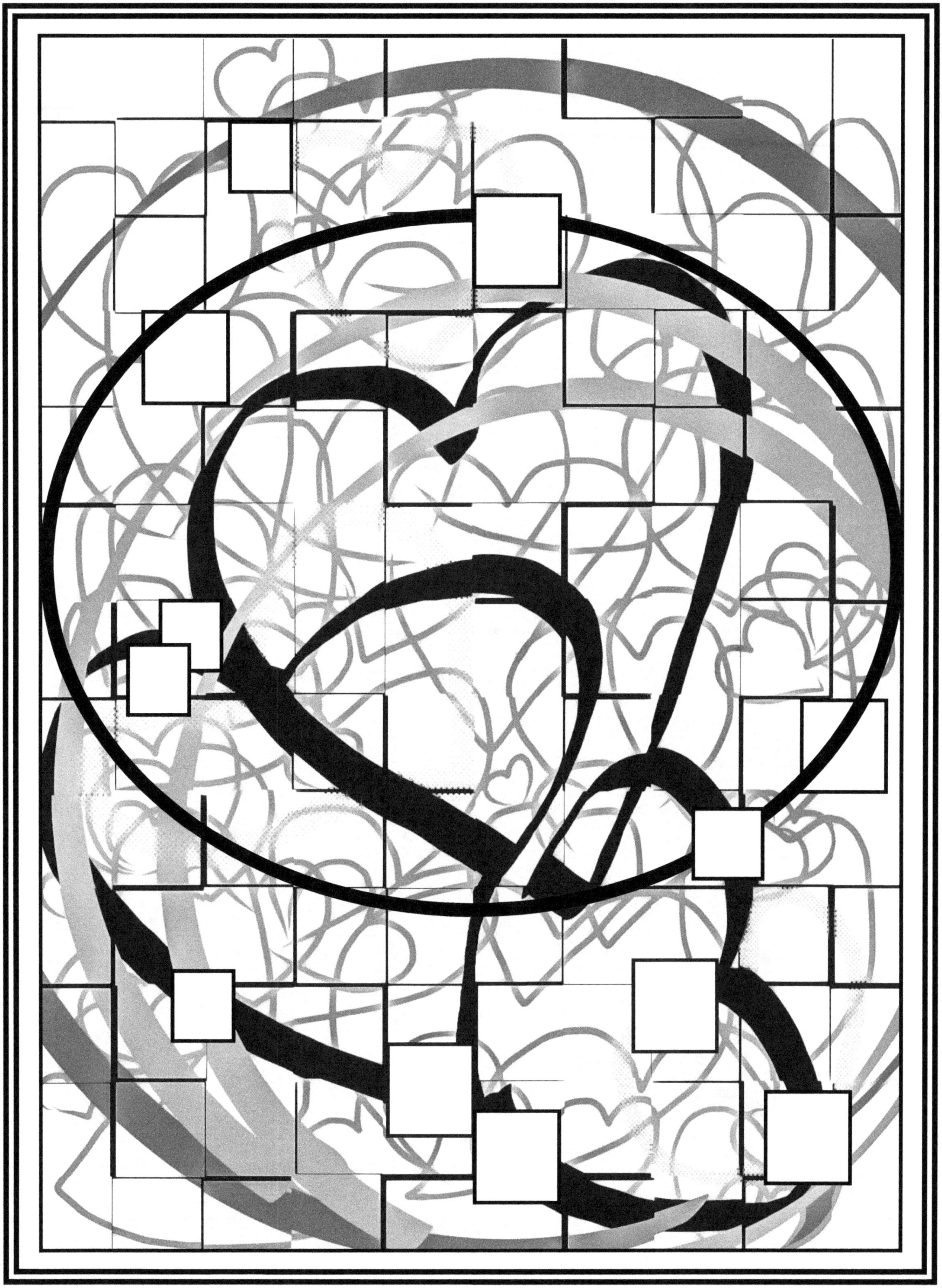

Other Print Books By
Curtis W. Jackson

My Anyway Possible Coloring Book (Lulu Books)

Second Chances Coloring Book (Blurb, Lulu Books)

Bay Shore Unfocused (Blurb)

Late Afternoon in the Hop and Bark Park (Lulu Books)

Wearing the Thought: A Collection of CW Jackson's Apparel Designs

Curtis on the News: 2008-2013, The Unfinished Chronicles (Barnes and Noble.com, Lulu Books)

57 Sections: A Book of Cartoons (Barnes and Noble.com)

www.ingramcontent.com/pod-product-compliance
Lightning Source LLC
Chambersburg PA
CBHW081312180526
45170CB00007B/2679
* 9 7 8 0 3 5 9 9 1 3 7 1 8 *